Invitation to
Presence

Invitation to Presence

A Guide
to Spiritual
Disciplines

Wendy Miller

UPPER
ROOM BOOKS
NASHVILLE

INVITATION TO PRESENCE
Copyright © 1995 by Wendy J. Miller
All rights reserved.

No part of this book may be reproduced in any manner whatsoever without written permission of the publisher except in brief quotations embodied in critical
articles or reviews. For information, address The Upper Room, 1908 Grand
Avenue, P.O. Box 189, Nashville, Tennessee 37202-0189.

Scripture quotations not otherwise identified are from the New Revised
Standard Version of the Bible, copyright 1989 by the Division of Christian
Education of the National Council of the Churches of Christ in the USA and are
used by permission.

Scripture quotations designated TEV are from the Good News Bible, The Bible
in Today's English Version—Old Testament: Copyright © American Bible
Society 1976; New Testament: Copyright © American Bible Society 1966,
1971, 1976.

Scripture quotations designated NEB are from the *The New English Bible*. © The
Delegates of Oxford Universtiy Press and The Syndics of the Cambridge
University Press 1961, 1970. Reprinted with permission.

Cover design: Gore Studio, Inc.
Interior design: C. Sutherland Book Designs
Cover photograph: © Annie Griffiths Belt/Woodfin Camp & Associates
First Printing: October 1995 (5)
ISBN: 0-8358-0738-3
Library of Congress Catalog Card Number: 94-60658

Printed in the United States of America

FOR

❀

Burt, Gerald, Kevin, Lawrence, and Shirley

*Pilgrims and partners, offering
an invitation to presence*

CONTENTS

INTRODUCTION

❀

As I wrote this book for persons wanting to learn more about prayer, I was very aware that I am still learning to pray. The word *learning* has various shades of meaning in our time. For me it can conjure up claims made by a computer company advisor who was selling his company's computers on the basis of the short "eight-hour learning curve" one needed to be able to use their product. The danger of a course in prayer is in our tendency to believe that a twelve-week learning curve will do it—we will then know how to pray. However, we will always be beginners in the experience of prayer.

While this idea of always being a learner may frustrate us, it can also free us from the trap of thinking that if we master the techniques, then we can make prayer work. Being learners frees us to be children as we pray. We can come simply as we are, with dirt on our face and knees. We can come trusting that we don't have to know it all.

I am aware as I write and teach about prayer that we may be wary of praying. On the one hand our experience of prayer may have been boring, distant, or painful. I remember as a child counting the colored pieces of stained-glass windows as I waited for prayers to end during worship and trying to stifle laughter (unsuccessfully) during closing prayers at Girl Scout meetings. I also remember weeping as I knelt beside my bed night after night, begging God to bring our family back together after my parents' divorce and thinking that my prayers went no further than the brass light fixture hanging from the ceiling.

So why learn to pray now? God surely is still boring and distant, and God does not magically take away the pain of family breakup. We may have some concern about venturing into the world of prayer and the Spirit. Will we be safe? There seem to be so many new and strange spiritualities on the horizon these days.

When I accepted the invitation from Upper Room Books to write this book, I kept these kinds of concerns in mind and decided to use the scriptures as a starting point in our journey of learning to pray. The early disciples (whose adventures with Jesus definitely were not boring, distant, or without pain) watched and listened as Jesus prayed. They later made a request: "Lord, teach us to pray" (Luke 11:1).

We are also learners. Jesus becomes our teacher. We can learn from the wisdom of other pilgrims who encountered God in prayer—in the Hebrew and New Testament Scriptures and in the community of faith we call the church. These teachers help us as they point us to some trusted ways into the field of God's presence. They also help us understand that prayer is not only talking to God, but prayer includes listening, seeing, and allowing our lives to be changed. Then we begin to connect learning to pray with what Jesus said the good news was about: the deaf being able to hear, the blind receiving their sight, and the lame walking.

I would like to express my warm thanks to the students and Formation in Personhood faculty at Eastern Mennonite Seminary in Harrisburg, Virginia. Their lively responses and helpful suggestions to this course on prayer grew out of their living with the text and from their experience of practicing the spiritual disciplines together and in solitude. My appreciation also goes to Heidi Miller Yoder, Amy Kuepfer, and Peggy Raboin for their skill and helpfulness in typing the manuscript and doing background research. My gratitude to the men and women whose personal stories this book includes—persons who are learning to pray and open their attention to the gracious and loving presence of God. I have changed names and identifying facts and shaped stories in order to preserve confidentiality, except where noted. Last and first, I'm thankful to my husband Ed for his patient, helpful, and gentle walking alongside as I wrote.

I write in memory of Paul Tournier, a physician and church

member in Switzerland who learned to pray, and from whose writings I also learned to open my attention to God—to listen, to see, and to allow the spirit of Jesus to walk into the world of my heart and life.

As You Use This Book

✿

Chapter 1 serves as an invitation to walk into the world of the heart, for this is where all prayer begins. The remaining chapters fall into two main parts: the first section, chapters 2–5, introduces us to the spiritual disciplines that help us listen on a heart level. The second section, chapters 6–10, focuses our attention on the spiritual disciplines that assist us to see with the eyes of the heart.

Each chapter's content includes the following outline:

Vignette: a contemporary story describing the experience of persons that connects with the prayer form in the chapter followed by a laying out of a contemporary problem.

✿ **WALK INTO THE FIELD:** An invitation to slow down, leave the path of our six-lane, fast-track living, and be receptive to what Jesus and other pilgrims in the scriptures and the faith community have to say about prayer.

Listening to Jesus (chapters 1–5)/**Seeing with Jesus** (chapters 6–10): An opportunity to be present along with the early disciples as Jesus leads us into the world of the heart through the use of parables, story, and conversation about prayer.

Digging Deeper: Some explanation of Jesus' teaching.

Listening with Others in the Faith Community

. . . in Hebrew Scriptures

Encounters with women and men in the Hebrew Scriptures who experience the presence of God as they pray and serve to illustrate the use of spiritual disciplines.

. . . in the New Testament community
Encounters with women and men in the community of the
New Testament church who open their attention to the presence of God as they pray and practice spiritual disciplines.
. . . in the church
An opportunity for us to learn from the gathered wisdom of
believers across the centuries as they develop and practice
the spiritual disciplines they discover in the scriptures.
Reflection: Each chapter includes several pauses, which
offer some guidance for reflection as you read.

❀ INVITATION TO PRESENCE
Practice the spiritual discipline: Information and guidance to assist you and others in a small group to experience
the prayer form taught in the chapter, to open your attention
to God.
Journaling: Some helpful guidance for reflecting on the
prayer experience.

❀ BACK ON THE PATH: some suggestions for continuing to
practice the spiritual discipline throughout the week, and to
be open and responsive to God's presence in all of life.

1

A Matter
of the
Heart

Pay attention to how you listen.
—Luke 8:18

I *first heard the parable stories*
while sitting in a circle with about
six other church school children
beneath the high windows of All Souls
Church parish hall in Eastbourne, a
coastal town in southern England. We fol-
lowed as our kind and patient teacher,
Miss Betty, led us along the paths and
beaches into the fields and houses of the
New Testament, always listening to what
Jesus had to say and noticing what he did.
For some reason or other, the parables
grabbed my attention, mostly because I
couldn't figure out what they meant. I
remember turning the parables over and
over in my mind as I walked home.

1

The net Jesus cast through those stories caught my imagi-
nation. They intrigued and puzzled me, tugging my thinking
to the limits of my understanding. Finally, I was content to turn
my young mind to other things. But my heart had been hooked.

❀

Only much later did I realize that this is precisely what Jesus
wants his teachings and stories to do—to catch our hearts and
minds in their net so that we are drawn up onto the beach where
he is sitting, welcoming us as we come. As we walk toward Jesus
we carry with us all that is in our heart and mind.

To help us understand this knowledge of the heart that Jesus
offers, the Gospel writers use words and images that invite us into
the world of Capernaum—a town that hugs the northern edge of
Lake Galilee. The people of Capernaum live in that narrow space,
between a hilly wilderness and the lake. Town, country, and fishing folk, they work, worship, marry, raise children, grumble about
the Roman occupation and taxes, and (for safety reasons) prefer
the broader trade routes running south when making pilgrimages
to Jerusalem to worship. Coping with the everyday demands of
life gives them plenty to talk about.

Of course there is the weather: an occasional drought that
causes food shortages or worse yet, one of those sudden storms
that swoops onto the lake—sinking boats, drowning fathers and
sons, wrecking a family business and income. Then in the dark
night of grief and loneliness, they worry about having enough
money to pay debts and further loss through a loved one's becoming ill. In the recesses of their hearts, they wonder how long they
will live before death takes them to the grave.

Into this narrow existence along the shore of Galilee, Jesus
has come and made his home: "In Capernaum by the sea, . . . the
people who sat in darkness have seen a great light, and for those

who sat in the region and shadow of death light has dawned" (Matthew 4:13, 16).

The Creator God who has spoken all of earth, sea, sky, and heaven into being, now walks this patch of beach in the person of his son, Jesus. Peter offers Jesus lodging at his house. This fishing family does not know who Jesus is; neither do the folk in Capernaum. Later John would write,

> He was in the world, and the world came into being through him; yet the world did not know him. He came to what was his own, and his own people did not accept him. But to all who received him, who believed in his name, he gave power to become children of God, who were born, not of blood or of the will of the flesh or of the will of man, but of God. And the Word became flesh and lived among us.
>
> —John 1:10-14

If we listen to the conversation among Jesus' disciples, we soon realize that he is no ordinary houseguest. Jesus tells stories at the table and invites children into the circle of adult conversation to receive a blessing. Jesus has a way of reminding high-minded grownups that children are our teachers when it comes to entering the kingdom of heaven, the home for which we long. Peter remembers how Jesus healed his mother-in-law who was in bed with a fever. Jesus also had showed his authority in the synagogue that day, ordering an unclean spirit to leave a man who began shouting in the middle of a sermon. Those standing by were astounded at his teaching, amazed at his authority, and "that evening at sundown, they brought to him all who were sick or possessed with demons. And the whole city was gathered around the door" (Mark 1:32-33).

As we listen, we realize that we may give Jesus a place to stay in a spare room, but the Lord of the universe is not content to be a quiet, unobtrusive guest. Soon he will attract people we would rather not touch or be seen with—the lepers of society who come with requests, "If you choose, you can make me clean." Jesus, moved with pity, stretches out his hand and touches them, saying, "I do choose. Be made clean!" (See Mark 1:40-44.) Then he begins explaining how they can be part of our community circle!

People will dismantle the protective roof of our house in order to get closer to this Jesus within, for they and their friends need healing too (Mark 2:1-12). Jesus breaks down walls of social stigma, enjoys partying with those who are politically left and right, defies laws and traditions that keep people hungry, ill, or outcast (Mark 2:13–3:6). We discover that Jesus relates to women with the power of respect and tenderness. He declares that they are full members of the household of God.

For men he models the greatness of servanthood; and if Jesus criticizes, he speaks out against "the very premises on which domination is based: the right of some to lord it over others by means of power, wealth, shaming, or titles."[1] And while the life of power and comfort draws us, Jesus' description of the kingdom draws our hearts:

> God's domination-free order . . . a message so elementary that even a small child can understand it. It means, for children, no more beatings; for women, no more battering and rape; for men, no more violence and war.[2]

Gradually we find ourselves reacting, *Is this man safe to have around?* Some are saying he goes too far, and they want Jesus out of the way (Mark 3:6). In our hearts we know we need his message, and not just we but the persons around us, the cities, the nations. And so we stay in spite of our fear and resistance as Jesus forthrightly recites a list of all the evil that we thought we had hidden safely in the basement of our heart-house: "From [your] heart come the evil ideas which lead [you] to kill, commit adultery, and do other immoral things; to rob, lie, and slander others" (Matthew 15:19, TEV).

Now that Jesus has seen behind the respectable paint-work and knows what goes on behind closed doors, we are astonished that he doesn't pack up his bags and leave. Instead he says that he wants to make his home with us, basement and all; and we know we are in the presence of a love we cannot fathom.

So we stay and listen, for we know that we need healing and hope for the lost and hidden places in the heart. We know we have to attend to a matter of the heart. We need healing; we need to enter the kingdom of heaven ourselves. So we stay and listen, standing on the beach by the sea at Capernaum along with the rest of the crowd.

To our surprise Jesus throws out a net of parables. The people had trusted their diseases and mental illness to Jesus. Now he wants to draw their hearts and ours into the kingdom. This net is not spun from an other-worldly yarn but from a sturdier fabric woven with the common threads of everyday life, knotted and dyed with stories about planting seeds, making bread, fishing, children who are disobedient, cleaning house, paying wages, getting lost and finding our way home.[3]

WALK INTO THE FIELD

❀

LISTENING TO JESUS

Jesus invites us to hear the parable of the sower and the seed:

Listen! A sower went out to sow. And as he sowed, some seeds fell on the path, and the birds came and ate them up. Other seeds fell on rocky ground, where they did not have much soil, and they sprang up quickly, since they had no depth of soil. But when the sun rose, they were scorched; and since they had no root, they withered away. Other seeds fell among thorns, and the thorns grew up and choked them. Other seeds fell on good soil and brought forth grain, some a hundredfold, some sixty, some thirty. Let anyone with ears listen!

—Matthew 13:3-9

At first hearing, the parable about a farmer's planting seed sounds as if Jesus is giving advice as to which kinds of soil will yield the most grain and what prevents the harvest. But if we delve a bit deeper into what Jesus is saying, we begin to realize that actually the story is about how we listen. Jesus begins and ends the story with instructions to listen, and so we listen with the disciples as Jesus explains the reason he uses parables: "It's because you have a heart condition. Your inner ears are deaf, and the eyes of your spirit cannot see." Jesus goes on to say, "Isaiah was right when he said,

'You will indeed listen, but never understand,
and you will indeed look, but never perceive.
For this people's heart has grown dull,
and their ears are hard of hearing,
and they have shut their eyes;
so that they might not look with their eyes,
and listen with their ears,
and understand with their heart
and turn—
and I would heal them.'

"But blessed are your eyes, for they see,
and your ears, for they hear."

—Matthew 13:14-16

DIGGING DEEPER

The shift from a deep-seated avoidance of encounter with God to a healing receptivity to God begins as we pay attention. Spiritual disciplines assist us to slow down, to hear, to pay attention, and then to listen for the word of God as it moves from our head into our heart. Once we understand on a heart level, we realize our need to turn to God to receive healing.

A journey on foot into the world of the heart requires a different kind of road map than we customarily use. The new technologies and gadgets, designed to enhance our lives, inundate us but

> the vaunted technologies of our day are used only along the shoreline of the human condition; the vast interiors are bereft. The consequence is that, lacking adequate tools, . . . most people don't venture into these interiors, at least not very far. Life is constricted on the boundary . . . where a narrow competence in doing and getting is exercised.[4]

Other companions on the inner way have charted maps for us from having walked the terrain of their own heart experience. These maps include the spiritual disciplines in this book. While the word *discipline* may strike a negative note for some, I invite you to bring to mind a fuller meaning of the word:

> We may be surprised at how many disciplines we use in a day in order to eat, travel, work, speak, and play. We are so used to measuring the coffee; we forget the discipline of learning how to use a measure. We hardly can remember the disciplines of counting and reading, although we read and use numbers every day. These disciplines are so much a part of us that we do not think of them as being difficult or getting in the way. Being able to read and count helps us to get where we need to go. And spiritual disciplines assist us in our receptivity to God.[5]

The spiritual disciplines are invitations to presence. The disciplines included in this book help us shift from listening and seeing in order to be receptive on a deeper heart level. We become open to the presence of God. Jesus knows us well, and beyond the physical ills which he came to heal, he sees our need of a healing of the heart. Isaiah foresaw Jesus' coming and wrote,

"Here is your God . . . .
    He will come and save you."
Then the eyes of the blind shall be opened,
    and the ears of the deaf unstopped;
then the lame shall leap like a deer,
    and the tongue of the speechless sing for joy.
                                                —Isaiah 35:4-6

Jesus allowed this portrait of his ministry to inform his life and work. Integral to the good news of salvation is the healing of our blindness and the enabling of our ears to hear. This inner healing frees us to walk and speak and sing—the marks of fruitful and faithful living.

LISTENING WITH OTHERS IN THE FAITH COMMUNITY

As you read this book, we are beginning a journey together. Our course will take us into the world of prayer with other travelers: men and women in the world of the scriptures and church history who were drawn to open their attention to God.

The destination of our journey is not to collect more information in order to function more efficiently in our six-lane, fast-track society, although we will learn together. Rather, we are responding to a yearning within our own hearts to walk slowly and listen deeply to those we meet. As we do, we enter the world of our own heart and come home to God's presence.

. . . in the Hebrew Scriptures
Throughout the Hebrew Scriptures we hear God's call: "Return to me with all your heart, . . . rend your hearts and not your clothing" (Joel 2:12, 13). But even as we long for peace and healing,

we fear exposing what is within us to God. The prophet Jeremiah tells us why: "The heart is devious above all else; it is perverse—who can understand it?" (Jeremiah 17:9). Part of our heart illness is our avoidance of the very One who can cure us. But even as we hide, God continues to offer comfort and healing: "A new heart I will give you, and a new spirit I will put within you; and I will remove from your body a heart of stone and give you a heart of flesh" (Ezekiel 36:26).

If we pause to listen to the heart prayers of these Hebrew pilgrims, we receive guidance for our own prayer of response to God's invitation for healing:

> Create in me a clean heart, O God,
>   and put a new and right
>   spirit within me.

> —Psalm 51:10

. . . in the New Testament community

Luke's Gospel offers us some quiet and solitude as Luke allows us to enter the stable and sit with Mary. Here Luke invites us to treasure the good news of Jesus' coming into our world, to ponder it in our heart (Luke 2:17-18).

John, Peter, and Paul give us permission to walk with them into the world of their heart and to reveal the struggle that occurs there. But even as they own their inner resistance to God, they also let us know that the good news brings peace and rest. John tells us we are "beloved" and accepted by God who is greater than the guilt and condemnation that our heart may churn up. (Read 1 John 3:19-20; 4:7, 9-10). After his denial of Jesus, Peter confesses that God knows him through and through; the Christian community affirms that God's love "covers a multitude of sins" (1 Peter 4:8).

Paul walks us into the war zone within and gives us an inside look at forces in the conflict:

I find it to be a law that when I want to do good, evil lies close at hand. For I delight in the law of God in my inmost self, but I see in my members another law at war with the law of my mind, making me captive to the law of sin that dwells in my members. Wretched man that I am! Who will rescue me?

—Romans 7:21-24

. . . in the church
Because we believe that we cannot earn God's work of rescuing us—it is a gift—we may slip into thinking that any effort on our part is an attempt to earn our salvation. If so, we can become suspicious of such practices as spiritual disciplines. However, while we know salvation is God's gift, we are called to grow "in love and prayer in the Christian life."[6] Jesus' invitation to pay attention to how we listen is also an invitation to allow the word God desires us to hear to descend from our minds into the heart. There it can become fruitful.

INVITATION TO PRESENCE

❀

PRACTICING: RECEPTIVE READING

To assist us in learning to listen as we read the scriptures, Robert Mulholland notes a difference between two kinds of reading.[7] For the most part in our high-tech information age, we read to obtain more information. Mulholland also explains a way to read for transformation. This kind of formative reading is a way of listening, of being present to the text. It is a basis for the practice of spiritual disciplines.

Informational Reading	Formational Reading
We cover as much as possible as quickly as possible.	We are not concerned with amount read, with "getting this book done." We are willing to wait before the text.
We move from a to b to c, in linear direction over the face of the text.	We read in depth, allowing the passage to open out to us in its multiple layers of meaning.
We exercise control through analysis, critique, passing judgment, organizing the content. We decide what is important, and how it is to be lined up. The text is the object over which we have control.	We are servants and become mastered by God who speaks through the word. Here we experience an open receptivity, a willingness for creation and formation of the new person in Christ.
We seek information to enhance our ability to function so as to change the world to our parameters.	The content serves to change the quality of our being. We become open to discover God's Reality— the kingdom of God, the "mind of Christ."
We come with a problem-solving mentality and read to find something that will work for us, fix what we are uncomfortable with.	We are receptive to the probing of the Holy Spirit, taking time to listen, to open to mystery.
We keep the text at a distance.	We are receptive to the Holy Spirit's shining the truth of God in the inner space within us—our heart space.
This involves human effort, analysis.	We receive Spirit gift, revelation.
Here we want to know.	Here we become known.

RECEPTIVE READING: READING FOR TRANSFORMATION

Formational reading asks us to stand still and be open to encounter as we listen to Jesus and the parable of the sower and the seed. The parable "is not an illustration to help [us] through a theological discussion; it is rather a mode of religious experience."[8] This kind of experience will challenge our compulsive need for control.

We need both kinds of reading as outlined by Mulholland. Phone directories, dictionaries, operator manuals, and cookbooks all help us function more efficiently in our world of print and technology. The danger is subtle, however. In our growing ability to obtain information through computer, laser, satellite and video technology, and a myriad of other services, we become more and more submerged in the worldview that tells us we are in control. We become blinded to the giftedness of all of life and to God's sustaining presence at the heart of who we are.

> Many of us and our congregations are guilty of "functional atheism." Though our language pays lip service to God, our actions assume that God does not exist or is in a coma. Functional atheism is the belief that nothing happens unless we make it happen. It is the belief behind our unwillingness to take solitude and silence seriously.[9]

In the following chapters we will explore the spiritual disciplines that help us deal with some of the blocks we encounter to listening with the heart—the rocks and the weeds of the parable. We will spend time in small groups,

✿ listening to one another's experience of the week;
✿ learning to hear and see with the heart as we experience new spiritual disciplines together.
And you will spend time alone,
✿ practicing the spiritual discipline(s) experienced in the group meeting;

❈   reading the chapter material for the next group meeting.

With other persons in and beyond the small group, you will
❈   pay attention to God's presence in all of life;
❈   live out the gospel in fruitful love and obedience to Jesus.

The Holy Spirit is present to help as we read and listen. John Wesley was aware of this need for prayerful waiting before the word of God and listening to the revelation given by the Spirit: "Serious and earnest prayer should be constantly used before we consult the oracles of God; . . . Scripture can only be understood through the same Spirit whereby it was given."[10]

ENDNOTES

1. Walter Wink, "The Kingdom: God's Domination-Free Order," *Weavings: A Journal of the Christian Spiritual Life* (January/ February 1995): 12.
2. Ibid., 15.
3. I am indebted for this way of seeing the parables to Megan McKenna, *Parables* (Maryknoll, NY: Orbis Books, 1994), 1.
4. Eugene Peterson, *Answering God: The Pslams as Tools for Prayer* (San Francisco, CA: HarperSanFrancisco, 1991), 2.
5. Wendy Miller, *Learning to Listen: A Guide for Spiritual Friends* (Nashville, TN: The Upper Room, 1993), 39.
6. Roberta C. Bondi, *To Pray and to Love: Conversations on Prayer with the Early Church* (Minneapolis, MN: Fortress Press, 1991), 50–51.
7. Adapted from M. Robert Mulholland, Jr., *Shaped by the Word* (Nashville, TN: The Upper Room, 1985), 47–60.
8. T. W. Manson quoted by Kenneth E. Bailey, *Through Peasant Eyes* (Grand Rapids, MI: William B. Eerdmans Publishing Company, 1980), xi.

9. Parker Palmer, "Born Again: The Monastic Way to Church Renewal," *Weavings: A Journal of the Christian Spiritual Life* (September/October 1986): 19-20.

10. John Wesley, *The Works of John Wesley*, 3rd ed. (Kansas City: Beacon Hill Press, 1979), XIV, 252f. Quoted by Mulholland, 166.

2

MAKING A TIME AND PLACE FOR GOD

*There are many ways of
"being" in a place.†*
Teresa of Avila

Be still, and know that I am God.
—Psalm 46:10

A pastor once told me about
his tendency toward preoccupation. He was walking
to his office at the church one morning, giving attention to the various
tasks of the day ahead. Without conscious awareness, he stepped over
hoses, walked around puddles of
water on the ground, maneuvered his
way among parked trucks and past
groups of persons beginning the
clean-up work. Only after he arrived
at his office and the church secretary
mentioned the fire that had burned
the Sunday school superintendent's
house next door during the night, did

he become aware of the event he had just walked through.

✬

Most of us can identify with this experience of closing ourselves off to what is around us because another compartment of time or concern is holding our attention. In my children's early years, I found myself engrossed in the endless tasks of home, work, parenting, cooking, and so on. Sometimes one of my children could stand beside me and call, and I would not hear my name. My attention was on the task at hand, or sometimes on the next three tasks to be done while I was immersed in another.

WALK INTO THE FIELD

✬

LISTENING TO JESUS

Jesus was aware of our tendency to be preoccupied, unaware, busy; unable to hear or to be present. At those times when a task engulfs us, and the demands of other requirements enslave our attention, we are not present to ourselves, others, or God. This kind of nonpresence can be a major stumbling block to opening our attention to God. Jesus draws our attention to our condition in his first part of the parable of the sower and the seed:

> Listen! A sower went out to sow.
> And as he sowed, some seeds fell on the path,
>   and the birds came and ate them up.

Later the disciples ask him what this parable means (Luke 8:9), and Jesus begins to unpack its meaning:

> Hear then the parable of the sower.
> When anyone hears the word of the kingdom
>   and does not understand it,

the evil one comes and snatches away
what is sown in the heart;
this is what was sown on the path.
—Matthew 13:3-4, 18-19

Reflection

Before reading further, let us acknowledge our need for help in understanding the kingdom. Pause now, and pray along with the pilgrims in Hebrew Scriptures. They also acknowledged their need for help in understanding what God was saying:

O God,
You created me, and you keep me safe;
    give me understanding . . .
I am your servant;
    give me understanding
    so that I may know your teachings.
—Psalm 119:73, 125, TEV

DIGGING DEEPER

Notice the path running alongside the field: a place for people to walk, their feet treading the earth into a hard crust as they make their way from one place to another, one task to another. As Jesus breaks open the meaning of the parable, he helps us understand that this pathway represents a way of hearing. The listeners give only their surface attention to the seed, the good news of God's gracious coming in Jesus. The hearers' preoccupation and lack of receptivity does not allow the word to penetrate. They do not understand the word, nor does it take root in their lives or bear fruit.

Jesus notes the evil intent that is at work here: "The evil one comes and snatches away what is sown in the heart." The result is a failure to hear or to understand what God is saying.

This problem is an old one that goes back to Eden. The serpent begins picking away at the experience and content of God's speech, first questioning what God has said, then denying that God has said it. The serpent sets a glittering snare of illusion and seduces the woman and the man, who become caught in its lies. We have been caught ever since.

We live most of our life oblivious to our true identity as persons created and provided for by God. We race around as if it were all up to us to make a living. And having made a living, we believe that what we earn and what we own is what gives us identity. Life ceases to be a gift. Instead, it is something we grasp, keep, protect, and fear losing. We run to and fro—always busy and never hearing—unaware that One who is infinitely greater and loving holds our lives.

Reflection
Reflect on your times of busyness and preoccupation, times when you possibly resist God's presence.

The parable is about listening, about being in the field. The seed will only grow if it gets planted in the field. If we are desiring more depth in our lives—a rootedness in the midst of a world that has lost its grounding in God—and a fruitful life that knows rest, satisfaction, and a giftedness for others, then we need to heed Jesus' words.

The psalmist knew of this same need, and prayed his/her experience of coming into the field of God's presence.

> The Lord is my shepherd; I have everything I need.
> He lets me rest in fields of green grass
>   and leads me to quiet pools of fresh water.
> He gives me new strength.
> —Psalm 23:1-3, TEV

Jesus describes himself as the good shepherd and invites us to listen for his voice: "He calls his own sheep by name and leads them, . . . and the sheep follow him because they know his voice" (John 10:3, 4).

The invitation here is to solitude and listening, to make a time and a place in our lives to be present and attentive to Jesus. Solitude is both a place apart and a place of stillness and presence for God within the heart.

As we are present to God in places of solitude away from the daily demands of work and needs of persons, gradually we notice God's presence within our work relationships. Our being present to God in solitude gradually transforms our fragmented life of rushing around from one thing to another into more of a coherent whole. We begin to realize that God is at work in us, and gradually our whole life embodies God's work in and through us.

Jesus developed a rhythm of finding places to pray early in his life. While still a child, he claimed the temple in Jerusalem as his Father's house and later declared it a place of prayer for all people (Mark 11:17). He sought out the solitude of early mornings in the wilderness, days on the mountains, evenings in a favorite garden, retreat on the lake, and an upper room to pray and reflect on God's purposes over meals.

While Jesus knew God was always present and always listening (John 11:41-42), he recognized his need for time away from others, from the voices and claims of work among the people. In the quiet of God's presence in solitude, he found fresh direction for the tasks at hand and was restored in his awareness of the care and sustaining love of God (Mark 1:33-39).

Jesus knows that we too need times and places for prayer:

> Whenever you pray, go into your room and shut the door and pray to your Father who is in secret; and your Father who sees in secret will reward you.
>
> —Matthew 6:6

LISTENING WITH OTHERS IN THE FAITH COMMUNITY

. . . in the Hebrew Scriptures

Behind and within the Hebrew narratives is the pervasive and passionate presence of Yahweh. The God who creates, loves, and sustains our life also comes looking for us, calling: "Where are you? . . . Listen carefully to me. . . . Incline your ear, and come to me; listen, so that you may live" (Genesis 3:9; Isaiah 55:2, 3). The stories of those who respond to God's invitation to presence lead us into the vast solitude of the desert. There Yahweh waits like a patient lover and husband, saying to his bride: "I will . . . bring her into the wilderness, and speak tenderly to her" (Hosea 2:14). Those who hear God in that wilderness solitude—Abraham and Sarah, Hagar, Jacob, Moses, the people of Israel, and others— become responsible for creating their own desert where they can pray. They choose places and times to be with God. These places for prayer include altars, wells, an open upstairs window, a tent, and houses for prayer and worship (Genesis 12:8; 13:4, 18; 26:23-25; 16:14; Exodus 35:4-5, 20-21; 1 Samuel 1:9, 10, 17; 1 Kings 5:2-5; 8:1, 10-13; Daniel 6:10).

A rhythm of times for prayer also emerges: the yearly festivals of Passover, Day of Atonement, and Harvest; the weekly day for sabbath rest; and the daily rhythms of prayer in the morning (Job 1:5; Psalm 5:3; 88:13; Isaiah 50:4), at noon (Psalm 55:17), evening (Ezra 9:5; Psalm 4:3), and at night (Psalm 63:5-7; 134:1).

. . . in the New Testament community

If we follow the early Christians, we will discover them at prayer in various places and at different times. They found an upstairs room conducive to prayer (Acts 1:13-14). The Temple offered a place to pray at regular times throughout the day (Acts 3:1). Prayer held a central place in their understanding of what it meant to be the church, both together (Acts 1:14; 2:42) and in solitude (Acts 9:11; 10:9).

. . . in the early church community

After two centuries of growth and expansion, accompanied by persecution leveled at the Christians by Jews and Romans, the Roman emperor Constantine finally declared that all the Roman world would be Christian. Believers in the church were no longer a separate group in a society that either ignored, admired, or persecuted them. Now all persons, no matter how shallow or nominal their belief, were swept into the church. In order to know how to live in the world that "rubber stamped" every person with the name of Christ, some believers retreated into the solitude of the desert to discover how to "live out fully what it means to be a Christian while trying to come to terms with a culture intent upon swallowing up Christian goals and values."[1] There they continued the pattern of private and communal prayer that the Christians of the first two centuries had followed.

> They prayed with the expectation that where two or three were gathered, there the Holy Spirit would be with them. . . . Even when praying alone they knew they prayed as part of the body of Christ. . . . They prayed facing east, toward the rising sun, at set times, between three and seven times a day. Their prayer was partly spontaneous, partly based in Scripture—the Psalms particularly, but the rest of the Old and New Testaments as well.[2]

The praying based in scripture grew out of drawing apart to listen for God's speaking the word to them. One of the desert fathers Abba Poemen believed in the slow but steady power of scripture to soften and heal our hearts:

> The nature of water is soft, that of stone is hard; but if a bottle is hung above the stone, allowing the water to fall drop by drop, it wears away the stone. So it is with the word of God; it is soft and our heart is hard, but the [person] who

hears the word of God often opens his [or her] heart to . . . God.[3]

Our prayerful listening to God softens the hard and busy paths that still crisscross our heart, kidnapping our attention away from God, others, and our most true self.

INVITATION TO PRESENCE

✸

PRACTICING: MAKING A TIME AND PLACE FOR GOD

This week you began exploring the place(s) and times that assist you to slow down and to open your attention to God.

Finding a Place

We can pray anywhere—God is always present. But in a crowded, busy world, space for God sometimes seems scarce. Finding a place to pray can be a first step in estab-lishing consistent prayer disciplines.[4]

Maybe you can arrange a room to include a place for prayer. Some persons need to be near a window or to be outside under the open sky with trees nearby; others enjoy the seclusion of a corner where they have set a chair, a small table, a lamp or candle, and possibly a piece of art or a plant that invites them to open their attention to God. One man I know found that working on a car (an ongoing odd job) for an hour after work in the solitude of his garage, was a conducive place and time to pray and respond to God's presence.

Choosing a Time

Choosing a time for prayer needs realistic reflection on our part. Begin noticing those times when you are awake, alert, and can schedule in some time for prayer and meditation. For some of us it is early in the morning; for others it will be after breakfast or at noon. One woman I know takes part of her lunch hour and goes to a quiet church to pray.

For a few years in my life when the children were smaller, I found that in the evening after they were all in bed was a good time for me to read and pray. Even if I could only spend fifteen minutes to a half hour in reading the scripture and in quiet reflection, I would have garnered some phrase or word to carry with me.

Opening Our Attention to God

As we come to a place and time for prayer, we often discover that we are full of activity and noise inside. Our body may be in place, but thoughts about what happened the day (or hour) before has captured our attention and led it off somewhere else. Maybe we repeat the conversation in our mind, or possibly we are rehearsing what we will say next. In any case, we are absent while present. As Teresa of Avila so rightly says, "There are many ways of 'being' in a place." To help us slow down, and to assist us in opening our attention for God, some simple exercises as we come to pray can be helpful.

Breathing

After sitting comfortably begin breathing slowly. Breathe in slowly, hold your breath for a second or two; then breathe out slowly. After exhaling, pause for a few moments; then inhale again slowly.

As you inhale, receive all that is of God; as you breathe out, release all that blocks your presence for God.

Repeat this slow, gentle rhythm of breathing five or six times.

Coming into God's presence

Hear Jesus speaking to you the words: *Come to me, all you that are weary and carrying heavy burdens, and I will give you rest.*

See yourself walking away from your workplace, your house, all that you are responsible for, and walking down a path toward a quiet place where Jesus is standing, waiting for you. Notice what you are carrying with you; as you come to Jesus, release it all in his presence. Hear him saying, "Take my yoke upon you and learn from me."

(The invitation to receive his yoke refers to the yoke the larger, more experienced ox would bear. Jesus represents the older, stronger ox, who bears the heavy end of the yoke.[5] He knows the direction to go, he knows the direction of the Lord of the field. Jesus invites us to shoulder the light end of the yoke, so that we will stay close to Jesus, moving where he walks, pausing when he stops.)

Resting the body

After sitting comfortably in a chair (or lying on the floor), pay kind attention to your body. Notice your feet, and appreciate how far they have walked today as they have taken you to the places you wanted to go. Relax and rest your feet now, as you are still. In the same way, now notice your legs, appreciate their strength to hold you up, to sit, to cradle a child. Relax and rest your legs now.

Our bodies are a gift from God, a dwelling place for God's presence, nurtured and sustained by God's care and provision. Pay attention to other parts of your body that may feel tense or tired: your back, your neck, your hands, your face. Relax any tension you feel, and appreciate the gift your body is to you.

Using a word from scripture

Choose one of the following short phrases from scripture. Say it slowly with as much attentiveness as possible. If you find busy thoughts distracting you, return to repeating the words and listening to their meaning:

Be still, and know that I am God.

—Psalm 46:10

The Lord is my shepherd, he gives me everything I need.

—Psalm 23:1

For God alone my soul waits in silence.

—Psalm 82:1

Using music

Some persons discover that instrumental music assists them in entering God's presence. For others, simply singing or humming a chorus or a hymn helps them lay down their busyness and open their attention to God.

JOURNALING

For some, journaling comes much more naturally than others. The important thing about journaling is that what we write (or draw) is honest and reflects in some way our experience in prayer—both our growth in openness and listening, and our resistance.

Notice those times and places when you become aware of God's presence this week. What do you notice about your response to God? Write a few sentences about what you are noticing in your journal.

BACK ON THE PATH

❀

Continue to spend time finding a place and time(s) for prayer and presence for God. Experiment with several of the exercises as you begin your time of prayer. Notice what assists you in your presence for God and what does not help you.

ENDNOTES

† Teresa of Avila, *Interior Castle*, translated and edited by Allison Peers (Garden City, NY: Image Books, 1989), 31.

1. Roberta C. Bondi, *To Pray and to Love* (Minneapolis, MN: Fortress Press, 1991), 17.
2. Ibid., 16.
3. Ibid., 86. See also *The Sayings of the Desert Fathers: The Alphabetical Collection.* Translated by Benedicta Ward, rev. ed. (Oxford: A. R. Mowbray, 1981), 192–3.
4. Marlene Kropf, "Learning to Pray: A Place to Pray," *The Mennonite*, 108:14 (July 27, 1993): 10.
5. I am indebted to Joe Haines, former missionary in Israel, for this understanding of the yoke Jesus offers us. (See Matthew 11:28-29.)

FOR FURTHER READING

Edwards, Tilden. *Sabbath Time: Understanding and Practice for Contemporary Christians.* Nashville, TN: Upper Room Books, 1992.

This spiritual formation classic invites readers to understand the sabbath as an alternative dimension for the Christian life, which maintains a balance between rest and vocation.

Harper, Steve. *Devotional Life in the Wesleyan Tradition.* Nashville, TN: The Upper Room, 1983.

Although Harper emphasizes a "devotional life" rather than a "devotional time," he notes that John Wesley's rule of prayer included private prayer (morning and evening), corporate prayer (morning and evening), audible and meditative prayer, written and spontaneous prayer. In chapter 2, Harper describes Wesley's private prayer life.

Nouwen, Henri J. M. *The Way of the Heart: Desert Spirituality and Contemporary Ministry.* New York: Harper Collins, 1991.
Nouwen looks to the desert fathers and mothers of the fourth and fifth centuries to learn how solitude, silence, and prayer can be part of our spirituality today.

3

Praying Our Experience

Save me, O God,
for the waters have
come up to my neck.
I sink in deep mire,
where there is no foothold.
—Psalm 69:1-2

*T*ravis had been married for twenty years and was the father of two teenage children. For some years, he had felt a vague sense of dissatisfaction within, even though he enjoyed teaching European history at a university and was happily married. He began to realize that his inner unrest was spiritual in nature, and for the last three years, Travis had begun praying and attending church. His wife, Alice, worked as a computer analyst for an international corporation and sometimes traveled on business trips. However, it was not her absences from home that caused Travis to seek pastoral *counseling but Alice's growing hostility about his faith in God. "She thinks I'm sort of simpleminded—not with it intellectually," he explained. "I'm finding that there's a real distance growing between us because I see God at the center of all of life. I don't talk about it much. It's not as if I'm trying to push religion or anything. But she just has no interest; and worse than that, she almost laughs whenever she finds me reading books on prayer. I guess it's the ridicule that's getting to me. At times I get really angry, and then I feel kind of lost and alone in my marriage. I'm not sure how to pray about something like this."*

✿

After hearing the results of a third series of medical tests, Ruth came to see me. Twenty-two years old and orphaned when she was ten, Ruth had begun attending church when she was twenty. Now that she knew her physical condition was inoperable, she began to talk with me about dying. One day she confessed that death was scary for her.

"Death is scary," I replied, "especially when you are only twenty-two." I remembered my own fears of the possibility of having cancer when I found a lump under my arm. I was thirty-two then and not ready to face my own mortality.

"I'm scared of what will happen," Ruth continued. "Especially since that time in the emergency room when my heart stopped." She recalled the dark, black sensation she had known during that near-death experience as a teenager.

"I'm afraid that's what it will be like forever," she was finally able to say. Ruth also realized she was avoiding speaking to God about her fears when she prayed.

Knowing that Ruth's faith in Jesus was new and sometimes fragile, I sensed she needed comfort on a deeper level

than any words I could say—some kind of consolation as she
walked through this difficult time. We turned to Psalm 23,
and I invited her to bring her present experience to the shep-
herd as she prayed the psalm.

"It's not just about resting in the field of the Good
Shepherd," I said, "but also about facing our dark fears
about death."

Ruth spent the next few weeks using the psalm during
her times of prayer. She also spent time in silence, learning
to wait in the presence of the Good Shepherd. Some time
later she told me that her attention had been drawn to the
field at the beginning of the psalm. In the field she was able
to experience the presence of Jesus, and for the first time she
brought her fears of death into her prayer. She began to
understand that death is not darkness but being in Jesus'
presence. Her fears began to lift.

WALK INTO THE FIELD

❀

LISTENING TO JESUS

Jesus is not a stranger to the belittling experience of Travis nor to
the feelings of abandonment in the face of death that Ruth knew.
In his hometown of Nazareth the people refuse to believe that
Jesus is anyone but a local boy making himself out to be someone
he is not. When he makes a home visit and teaches in their synagogue, the people are jealous and distrustful, and they reject him.
(See Mark 6:1-6.)

When Jesus heals a man who has lost the use of his right
hand, the religious leaders turn against him because he breaks
their tradition of the sabbath. (See Matthew 12:9-14.) At his
arrest, Jesus' disciples abandon him, and Peter denies even know-

ing this man. On the cross as he dies, Jesus feels alone and abandoned—even by God.

Jesus is intimate with our experiences of pain, loss, hostility, and abandonment. He knows how those adversities trouble our heart. In the parable of the sower and the seeds, he invites us to pay attention to what happens within us when suffering strikes:

> Other seeds fell on rocky ground, where they did not have much soil, and they sprang up quickly, since they had no depth of soil. But when the sun rose, they were scorched; and since they had no root, they withered away.
>
> —Matthew 13:5-6

To give us some guidance as to the meaning of the story, Jesus then goes on to say,

> As for what was sown on rocky ground, this is the one who hears the word and immediately receives it with joy; yet such a person has no root, but endures only for a while, and when trouble or persecution arises on account of the word, that person immediately falls away.
>
> —Matthew 13:20-21

DIGGING DEEPER

In the Shenandoah Valley in Virginia where I live, some fields are full of stones and rocks and are unusable for planting crops. Grasses and weeds and the occasional wild flower grow, but wheat or corn do not grow. Jesus saw fields like that in Palestine.

Jesus also sees the rocky circumstances that undermine our resources, trapping roots of faith and trust in a vicelike grip of worry and fear. At these moments, we tend to lose sight of God's good love and presence. We do not turn to God for help.

In the parable's explanation, Jesus speaks about two kinds of life events that tend to trap us in their powerful grasp, robbing us of faith, hope, and a sense of God's loving presence.

First Jesus mentions troubles, the difficulties and hardships that are part of our lives. We bear responsibility for some of the troubles, and others just happen. While we have a reasonable amount of control over how a car runs, it is still a piece of machinery. Automobiles wear out and inevitably need repair or replacement. If finances are tight because a family member needs extra medical treatment, or if the primary wage earner has been laid off work, then car repairs or buying a new vehicle can look like a mountain we are unsure of climbing.

In our anxiety and panic, we may well forget to pray, or we may see God as unfair, allowing bad things to happen to good people. And who wants to trust in a God like that? Ruth had no choice about being orphaned or being terminally ill. For Ruth, learning to trust God was full of difficulty and doubt because both her parents had abandoned her through death, and now illness was claiming her life. Although her small group at church had become a family in a very real sense, at times she forgot that and wondered if anyone really cared.

The book of Hebrew hymns and prayers that we call Psalms records this experience of losing sight of God's love. Persons coming to the temple or synagogue to pray were given words to voice their feelings. The psalms helped them pray their experience:

> There's nothing in life that's not in the psalms. They aren't all "nice" prayer. Some express anger. Some challenge God. Some are full of grief. Some are happy. Some ponder mysteries we don't know how to deal with: Why do the wicked prosper? Why do the innocent suffer? This gives the psalms a wholeness, a completeness, an aptness for any Christian's life. . . . In addition, the images, the emotions and the life in the psalms are available to everyone.[1]

Some of us may need courage to tell God how bad life is and just how we feel about it, especially if we have been schooled into

believing that God only listens to us if we are polite, have victorious faith, or only say what is positive and acceptable in prayer.

Having been raised under Victorian rules of behavior and
discipline, I was quite sure God would not listen if I said how I
really felt! After all, no other authority figure (except one kind
high school principal) had ever permitted me to speak my heart-
felt feelings. The first time I dared to let my fear, disappointment,
and anger spill out in prayer, I was sure God would do something
awful in return. To my surprise, I discovered that God listened
and even spoke comfort to my fearful heart.

Reflection
Listen to a lament from the Psalms:

> How long, O Lord?
>> Will you forget me forever?
> How long will you hide your face from me?
> How long must I bear pain in my soul,
>> and have sorrow in my heart all day long?
>>>> —Psalm 13:1-2

In what ways does this Hebrew prayer speak and give words to
your experience (now, or at some other time in your life)?

Second, Jesus speaks of persecution. He is addressing the kind of
suffering we experience when other persons harass and criticize
our faith in God, our belief in the good news of Jesus. Rather than
being welcomed and embraced by the community—whether our
family or some other group of people—we may experience rejec-
tion, mockery, or even physical abuse. Being ignored and treated
like a nonperson is just as painful.

But Jesus says there will be pain. Obedience to Christ is
costly. Rather than giving us a winning lottery ticket, Jesus offers
us a cross to carry. Through the loneliness within his marriage,
Travis is discovering the cost of obedience. His wife, Alice, does

not appear ready to believe that there is a God who initiated, created, and sustains all creation. She seems to live within the narrow confines of a materialistic worldview that rules out any dependence on or appreciation for God.[2] To Alice, Travis is a fool to trust in what you cannot prove. Sometimes her disdain gets to him.

LISTENING WITH OTHERS IN THE FAITH COMMUNITY

... in the Hebrew Scriptures

As we walk through the scriptures, we can hear persons praying in the midst of trouble and pain—Abraham's questioning God about being childless when God's promises depended on his having a son (Genesis 12:2; 15:1-3). In the wilderness of Sinai we find Moses, arguing with God about going back to Egypt (Exodus 3–4). Later we find Moses complaining long and hard to God (who was the food manager) when the people get fed up with having only manna on their menu (Numbers 11:5-15). In Shiloh we overhear Hannah praying out of her distress because she is childless. Shamed and harassed by a rival wife who has children, Hannah pours out her anxiety and vexation to God in prayer (1 Samuel 1:10). Praying her experience included bringing her feelings, her needs, and her desires to God. In Beersheba we hear Elijah telling God that he wants to die because of the queen's threats to his life.

As we stop to worship in the temple, we discover that the Hebrew hymnbook encourages such outbursts of anger, fear, and complaint. Over half of its contents are prayers and songs that help us give voice to the feelings hidden in the recesses of our heart.

> Why, O Lord, do you stand far off?
> Why do you hide yourself in times of trouble?
> —Psalm 10:1

> Save me, O God,
> for the waters have come up to my neck.
> I sink in deep mire,
> where there is no foothold;
> I have come into deep waters,
> and the flood sweeps over me.
>
> —Psalm 69:1-2

Look . . . and see—there is no one who takes notice of me; . . . no one cares for me (Psalm 142:4).

Jesus also prays out of his experience as he faces death on the cross. Deeply grieved and agitated, he throws himself on the ground saying, "My Father, if it is possible, let this cup pass from me" (Matthew 26:39).

On the cross Jesus prays the psalms, lamenting his experience of alienation and loss: "My God, my God, why have you forsaken me?" (Psalm 22:1; Matthew 27:46).

Then, just as he is about to die, Jesus prays a prayer of trust: "Into your hands I commit my spirit" (Psalm 31:5; Luke 23:46).

Reflection
Listen prayerfully to any pain or anxiety you discover in your own heart.

. . . in the New Testament
Sometimes we are too frightened to talk, too ashamed to voice our pain and our need. A woman who had suffered from hemorrhages for twelve years felt unable to tell Jesus about her experiences. The Jewish law labeled a woman with such an illness, as well as anyone who touched her, as unclean (Leviticus 15:25-30). She was an untouchable. In her poverty (for she had spent all she had on many physicians) and alienation, she approaches Jesus. Hoping to remain unseen, she comes up behind Jesus and touches the fringe of his clothes (Luke 8:43-48). To her joy, she is

healed. And to her shock, Jesus turns and asks who has touched him. In his kind presence, she is able to tell her story, to pray her experience. And in return, Jesus restores her to community saying, "Daughter, your faith has made you well; go in peace."

I believe we need to restore places for prayer in our houses of worship—places where we can come and be silent, yet in that silence touch the holy with our lament and need. Perhaps later we will have the freedom and courage to say our experience aloud.

Mary and Martha lamented their brother's illness and death. They shared their grief with Jesus when he arrived in Bethany. Even as he comforts them with the good news of death's giving way to his life and resurrection, he knows the groanings of the present time and weeps with them. (Read John 11:33-35; Romans 8:18-27.)

In the face of arrest and orders from the Jewish leaders not to speak about Jesus, Peter, John, and the other believers living in Jerusalem pray their experience of being threatened and ask God for courage to be faithful and obedient as God's servants. (See Acts 4:23-31.)

Paul, imprisoned because of his faithfulness to the gospel, writes a letter to the believers in Philippi. Out of his own experience of living on the edge of life and death, he invites these men and women to notice when they are worried and, in the midst of their anxiety, to turn to the Lord who is near (Philippians 4:5-7). He tells them that in praying their experience and asking for the help they need, a shift can happen. Thanksgiving, peace, and protection will begin to surround their troubled and frightened hearts, and they will know they are safe in the greater sustaining of the Lord Jesus.

As we come to prayer, we need the help of the Holy Spirit who helps us in our weakness; for we do not know how to pray as we ought, but that very Spirit intercedes with sighs too deep for words. And God, who searches the heart, knows what is the mind of the Spirit, because the Spirit intercedes for the saints [believers] according to the will of God.

—Romans 8:26-27

The spirit of Jesus indwells us: walking throughout our heart-space; seeing what traps us, engulfs us; knowing our experience of pain, fear, alienation, grief, anger, and loss of presence to God. In the midst of our experience, the Spirit begins helping by sighing our pain. And God, who sees all of our story, all that is happening within us, can interpret the sighs of the Spirit on our behalf. As we turn to God in the midst of our trouble, it is because the Spirit who lives within us helps us turn, even if all we are able to pray is a sigh.

INVITATION TO PRESENCE

❦

PRACTICING: PRAYING OUR EXPERIENCE

We may discover that the thrust of certain troubles catapults us into praying our experience without any thought of preparation. We are not quiet, open, ready to listen. But we are yelling for help in God's direction like a little child who cries out to his or her parent because of fear and danger.

At other times, as we come to our place of prayer and open our attention to God, we are ready to notice the tense times of the day (or of some other day) and to begin unloading our hearts' burdens in God's presence.

Use the words of a psalm. You may discover that the psalms express your feelings, your experiences. If so, then pray the psalms, staying with the words and phrases that embody your pain, your experience. Do not feel that you need to pray the whole psalm. This week, choose one or more of the psalms below (or another of your own choosing) to pray:

> O Lord, how many are my foes!
>   Many are rising against me;
> many are saying to me,
>   "There is no help for you in God."
> Selah
> [*be still and reflect on what you have just said*]
>
> But you, O Lord, are a shield around me,
>   my glory, and the one who lifts my head.
> I cry aloud to the Lord,
>   and he answers me from his holy hill.
> Selah
>
> —Psalm 3:1-4

> Save me, O God,
>   for the waters have come up to my neck.
> I sink in deep mire,
>   where there is no foothold;
> I have come into deep waters,
> . . . .
> My eyes grow dim
>   with waiting for my God.
> . . . .
> My prayer is to you, O Lord.
>   At an acceptable time, O God,
>   in the abundance of your
>   steadfast love, answer me.
> With your faithful help rescue me
> from sinking in the mire.
>
> —Psalm 69:1-3, 13

How long, O Lord? Will you forget me forever?
How long will you hide your face from me?
How long must I bear pain in my soul,
    and have sorrow in my heart all day long?

· ·

But I trusted in your steadfast love;
    my heart shall rejoice in your salvation.

—Psalm 13:1-2, 5

Protect me, O God, for in you I take refuge.
I say to the Lord, "You are my Lord;
    I have no good apart from you."

—Psalm 16:1-2

To you, O Lord, I lift up my soul.

· ·

Turn to me and be gracious to me,
    for I am lonely and afflicted.
Relieve the troubles of my heart,
    and bring me out of my distress.
Consider my affliction and my trouble,
    and forgive all my sins.

· ·

    for I wait for you.

—Psalm 25:1, 16-18, 21

Or pray in your own words. Either in verbal or written words, or in your journal (or you may want to draw), tell God about where you are in your life. Know that God is listening, understanding how you feel, and not rejecting your feelings or the words you use. Simply say it as it is for you.

    One man who decided to pray his experience of frustration with a decision affecting his job, began by saying to God:

I'm afraid to confront you with it
  I feel it strongly
    but can I express it?
To do so
  seems so much like rebellion
    it's not submission anyway.

But in your word
  I am encouraged
    by the God-wrestlers,
Encouraged
  to voice my complaint
  to cry out my pain.
So here goes
. . . .
This is my complaint
  God
Please don't file it somewhere.[3]

Catherine J. Foote, a minister to adolescents and their families, helps persons who have been abused to pray their experience:

God, I just want to talk to you. I just want to open my
soul to you. I don't want to try to say it right. I
don't want to meet someone else's expectations of what I
should say or what I should believe.
I just want to talk to you.
I sit sometimes in a deep well. I can't get out. I'm
so tired of the struggle. I ache.[4]

What do I dare tell you, God?
What do I dare to talk to you about?
May I speak of my anger? May I tell you of my shame?
Do you want to hear about the ugliness of the assault,
of all the ways it robbed me of my life?

Do you want to know about the confusion,
the betrayal?[5]

Be still and notice. After praying your story, whether through the
psalms or in your own words, allow the feelings to flow. Then be still.

Notice any slight movement of change, any invitation of
God, any beckoning of your attention in another direction. A
chapter or a book title may come to mind, a verse of a hymn or a
chorus. Sometimes we hear words of scripture being spoken to us,
sometimes other words come—clear and quiet and speaking comfort. Sometimes we are just still, tired after emptying everything
out but with some assurance that we have been heard.

Notice, and respond. God may be guiding you in some way
to a place where you will receive additional help.

JOURNALING

In your journal, write (or you may want to draw) and tell God
about where you are in your life. Know that God is listening,
understanding how you feel, and not rejecting your feelings or the
words you use. Simply tell it like it is for you.

Also consider recording a few sentences in your journal
about your experience of praying, lamenting.

BACK ON THE PATH

✸

This week notice the difficult and anxious moments: when you
are tired, angry, anxious, lonely, disappointed, grieving. When
you are able, open your attention to God and bring your experience into God's presence.

ENDNOTES

1. "Irene Nowell on Praying the Psalms," an interview by Art Winter. *Praying* (May/June 1993): 24.
2. Walter Wink, "Our Stories, Cosmic Stories, and the Biblical Story." "In this view, there is no heaven, no spiritual world, no God, no soul; there is nothing but material existence and what can be known through the five senses and reason. . . . The materialistic worldview, which has penetrated deeply into our culture, causes many to ignore the spiritual dimensions of life and the spiritual resources of faith." In *Sacred Stories: A Celebration of the Power of Story to Transform and Heal*, eds. Charles Simpkinson and Anne Simpkinson (San Francisco: HarperSanFranciso, 1993), 211.
3. David Gullman, Excerpt from "Wrestling with God," from his unpublished collection *My Life Prayers*. Used by permission.
4. Catherine J. Foote, *Survivor Prayers: Talking with God about Childhood Sexual Abuse* (Louisville, KY: Westminster/John Knox Press, 1994), 25.
5. Ibid., 5.

FOR FURTHER READING

Brueggemann, Walter. *Praying the Psalms*. Winona, MN: Saint Mary's Press, 1993.

Brueggemann invites the reader to pray the psalms as a way of expressing his or her life experience.

Foote, Catherine J. *Survivor Prayers: Talking with God about Childhood Sexual Abuse*. Louisville, KY: Westminster/John Knox Press, 1994.

A collection of prayers and meditations prayed by survivors of sexual abuse. For Foote, telling God the truth is a primary way of healing.

Peterson, Eugene H. *Answering God: The Psalms as Tools for Prayer.* San Francisco: HarperSanFrancisco, 1991.

A book to help us pray "with our eyes open, wide open."

Schmidt, Joseph F. *Praying Our Experiences.* Winona, MN: St. Mary's Press, 1989.

A book that "assures us that every aspect of life can be an occasion for turning to God."

4

MEDITATING ON SCRIPTURE

Let everyone who is thirsty come
Let anyone who wishes take the
water of life as a gift.
—Revelation 22:17

*I*t was the Sunday after New
Year's Day, the first week of
Epiphany in the church year,
and traditionally a day for remem-
bering the visit of the wise ones who
came to worship Jesus and bring
him gifts. Penny decided to open the
Sunday school class discussion by
asking the fifth and sixth graders to
talk about the custom of giving gifts
for Christmas.

"I like getting gifts," Sue said.
"But when I heard what some of the
other kids at school got, I didn't feel
so good. Jason said he got a TV and
VCR for his room, so now he can play
video games as much as he wants.

*After that I felt a bit dorky saying that my mom and dad had
given me new jeans and a sweater."*

*"I know what you mean," chimed in Brad. "My broth-
er told me that a girl in his senior class got a sports car from
her folks for Christmas—with the keys in it!"*

"Lu–cky!" wowed Tom. "They must be rich!"

"Wish my folks were that rich," Tracy sighed.

*Penny waited for a few moments, giving time for any-
one else who had something to say to enter the conversation.
But she sensed that Tracy's wish had struck a note that was
still echoing in the minds of the class. Discerning that this
could be a teachable moment to help the children consider
riches from God's perspective, Penny asked quietly, "What
do you mean when we talk about being rich?"*

❀

Penny knew that many voices claim our attention, informing us of
what will make us rich, powerful, in control. Her decision to help
the children reflect on their understanding of being rich was
prompted by her own awareness of those voices.

> Each day our society bombards us with a myriad of images
> and sounds. Driving . . . downtown . . . is like driving
> through a dictionary: each word demanding our attention in
> all sorts of sizes and colors and with all sorts of gestures and
> noises. The words yell and scream at us: "Eat me, drink me,
> buy me, hire me, look at me, talk with me!"[1]

For the fifth and sixth graders in Penny's class, hearing about the
expensive gifts that other children and teenagers had received was
the message: "You are only rich if you have what those other kids
have."

Walk into the Field

❀

Listening to Jesus

Jesus knows how many voices in the world inform us of what makes us wealthy, popular, right, "in," "out," secure. He sees how we spend much of our energy in that narrow strip of life between the wilderness and the lake, attempting to be "in" with the powerful and the beautiful in our own local Capernaum. Hence the third part of the parable: "Other seeds fell among thorns, and the thorns grew up and choked them" (Matthew 13:7).

> As for what was sown among thorns, this is the one who hears the word, but the cares of the world and the lure of wealth choke the word, and it yields nothing.
>
> —Matthew 13:22

Notice where the seed falls in the field: among thorns. The thorny plants also had found fertile soil and had begun putting down their roots before the other seed was planted. This head start gives the thorns an advantage, and in time they rob the fledgling seeds of light, moisture, and room to grow. In this way weeds can take over a whole section of a field, killing the harvest.

Jesus explains what it is that holds prior claim in our heart, gradually choking off the life and freedom that the Good News brings: the anxiety that permeates the world's system and our desire for things.

Digging Deeper

. . . Anxiety

Anxiety drives much more of our activity than we care to admit. For the most part we worry about losing: losing face, losing friendship, losing our health, losing a job, losing power, losing a grade, losing our youth, losing control, losing an investment.

Insurance and advertising companies make a great deal of money on our anxieties. Education, politics, and our church life are also places of anxiety-driven decisions, causing us to compromise our trust in the larger reality of the loving care and provision of God. We begin to forget who gives us our true identity. We choose to hold tightly to the identity of our own making as a protection against loss of popularity with others.

On the home front, I can identify with other homemakers who try to keep their house looking like a photo out of a glossy magazine. It took me a little while in the early years of keeping house to realize that picture-perfect for a women's journal is one thing; real life in motion is messy. The voices of magazines are powerful, causing anxiety in the heart of many a homemaker—especially if company is about to arrive.

My mother-in-law's gentle voice spoke a wiser message.

"Sit down and let's visit some," she would say. "I can always do those dishes after you leave. And as for the children's handprints on the windows, I don't like to wash them off for a while because they are beautiful. People are always more important than housecleaning."

The Gospel writers allow us to eavesdrop on a tense moment that occurs in the home of two sisters who invite Jesus and his disciples to stop by:

> Now as they went on their way, he entered a certain village, where a woman named Martha welcomed him into her home. She had a sister named Mary, who sat at the Lord's feet and listened to what he was saying. But Martha was distracted by her many tasks; so she came to him and asked, "Lord, do you not care that my sister has left me to do all the work by myself? Tell her then to help me." But the Lord answered her, "Martha, Martha, you are worried and distracted by many things; there is need of only one thing.

Mary has chosen the better part, which will not be taken away from her."

—Luke 10:38-42

The story has many layers, including Jesus' acceptance and defense of women who desire to listen as disciples,[2] but we cannot overlook the content of Jesus' exchange with Martha. Driven by her desire to prepare everything possible for her guests, Martha begins to feel anxious and alone in the midst of the many tasks she laid on herself to do.

Finally, full of worry, self-pity, and anger, she explodes into the room where Jesus is teaching and demands that he order Mary to help her. Jesus calls Martha's name twice, gently drawing her attention away from the voice of her expectations and toward what he knows she needs to hear: "Martha, Martha, you are anxious and distracted about many things, but there is one thing you need. Mary has chosen that one thing, to listen to me, Jesus, and it won't be taken away from her."

Jesus' intent is not to criticize or demean the need for food and hospitality. Rather, Jesus helps Martha become aware of what is driving her and of her anxiety, which finally erupted into anger and demand. Jesus invites her to realize that she also needs to sit still and listen to him. Then her work of hospitality would emerge out of love and simplicity, rather than the drivenness of many demands. Teresa of Avila, a woman who brought prayer and service into harmony in her life, reminds us: "We should desire and engage in prayer, not for our enjoyment, but for the sake of acquiring this strength which fits us for service."[3]

Reflection
Reflect on those times when you are aware of being anxious while you work.

What do you sense is the cause of your anxiety?

Allow Jesus' words to Martha invite you to listen to Jesus.

. . . Desire for things

Within the continent of our heart is the equivalent of a black hole, one of those celestial regions with an intense gravitational field. Believed to be a collapsed star, these holes suck everything into their dark space with a never-ending pull into extinction. James, writing about the desire within us that gives birth, grows, then collapses like a star into extinction, says,

> One is tempted by one's own desire, being lured and enticed by it; then, when that desire has conceived, it gives birth to sin, and that sin, when it is fully grown, gives birth to death.
> —James 1:14, 15

Our consumer society partially constructs itself on our dissatisfaction with what we have and our desire for something else. We recognize the sales pitch, "If they don't need it, create a need for it, then they will buy it." The more we buy, the more space we need to house, store, display what we have. And the more time and equipment we need to care for what we have. The result is little space, energy, or time for listening to God who satisfies all our deepest longings. As Augustine reminds us: "Thou has made us for thyself, and our souls are restless until they find their rest in Thee."

The weeds in the field rob the new seed of what they need to live and bear fruit: light, water, and air. Nothing else can satisfy the endless gasping for their deepest and truest need. God created plants in that way. And so it is with us. We can never satisfy the desire within us that craves everything under the sun, for it arises from within our false, constricted self. This false self is blind and deaf to the true needs within us and grasps continually for anything it desires to satisfy what can never be satisfied. Deeper within us is our true self, overpowered by the false. Paul, as he explored the continent of his heart, discovered

> I know that nothing good dwells within me, that is, in my
> flesh. I can will what is right, but I cannot do it. For I do not
> do the good I want, but the evil I do not want is what I do.
> —Romans 7:18-19

We find ourselves caught in this human dilemma—trapped by the weeds within our own heart field. Who can set us free? Paul, who admits he is a captive to the law of sin present within him, cries out, "Wretched man that I am! Who will rescue me from this body of death? Thanks be to God through Jesus Christ our Lord!" (Romans 7:24-25)

The Spirit of life in Christ Jesus comes to indwell us and set us free (Romans 8:2). The first step to freedom is becoming aware of the weeds.

The risen and glorified Jesus instructs John to write letters to seven congregations, one of which was in Laodicea. A center of banking and industry, the residents of that city could finance their own rebuilding when a severe earthquake hit that region of Asia Minor (modern-day Turkey) in A.D. 60. Laodicea was also famous for its black woolen cloth used for clothing and carpets, as well as having a medical school with its own brand of salves for the healing of ears and eyes. Church members saw themselves as rich, prosperous, and in need of nothing. Their prosperity filled the field of their vision, leaving Jesus outside the scope of their attention.

To this indifferent, nominal, and complacent congregation, the risen Christ brings an invitation (after a few wake-up words to get their attention!). He asks them to look beyond their narrow, little reality and see themselves within the Greater Reality of God. Jesus asks them to see that he asks admission of each individual in the church. The answer to their blindness, nakedness, and poverty is not another series of meetings or another program but an opening to presence: letting Jesus in. "Listen! I am standing at the door, knocking; if you hear my voice and open the door, I will come in to you and eat with you, and you with me" (Revelation 3:20).

"A shared meal in the ancient Jewish world had far more significance than it has today. It was a symbol of affection, of confidence, of intimacy."[4] Jesus invites us to open ourselves to his presence. In that presence we listen to him and then respond.

Reflection
Take some time to listen to Jesus' knocking, his asking you to open the door of your attention, and his expressing his desire to sit down with you at the table.

LISTENING WITH OTHERS IN THE FAITH COMMUNITY

. . . in the Hebrew Scriptures
The Hebrews acknowledged their ingrown hearing problem when it came to listening to God—not just on a surface level—but with the heart. Isaiah the prophet reports on how God sees those who treat prayer and worship as a religious routine:

> These people draw near with their mouths
>   and honor me with their lips,
>   while their hearts are far from me,
>   and their worship of me is a human commandment
>   learned by rote.

> —Isaiah 29:13

The psalmist uses some vivid language to explain how God remedies this problem in those who begin to open their attention to the Lord:

> You do not want sacrifices and offerings;
>   you do not ask for animals
>   burned whole on the altar
>   or for sacrifices to take away sins.

> Instead, you have given me ears to hear you. . . . .
> I keep your teaching in my heart.
>
> —Psalm 40:6, 8, TEV

Being able to "hear" so that we understand what God is saying, is God's gift. Understanding and insight signal the presence of God; God gives us ears to hear. Isaiah also speaks of this experience of God's being present and opening his ears:

> The Lord God has given me the tongue of
>   a teacher,
> that I may know how to sustain
>   the weary with a word.
> Morning by morning [God] wakens—
>   wakens my ear
>   to listen as those who are taught.
> The Lord God has opened my ear.
>
> —Isaiah 50:4-5

Not only did the Jews listen to God, but they meditated on what they heard being spoken, waiting for God to unfold a deeper meaning within their heart's understanding. The writers of the Hebrew prayer book insert the word *Selah* alongside the text to draw attention to how the words are to be said or sung, and invite the person praying the psalm to pause and lift the attention of their heart to what has just been prayed. [5]

As we leaf through the prayers of this extraordinary book of psalms, we hear the Jews' praying for God to give understanding:

> Make me understand the way of your precepts,
>   and I will meditate on your wondrous works . . . .
> I run the way of your commandments,
>   for you enlarge my understanding . . . .
> The unfolding of your words gives light;
>   it imparts understanding to the simple.
>
> —Psalm 119:27, 32, 130

They begin speaking the words with the mouth, in the awareness that as they repeat the words in the mind, their meaning sinks to a deeper heart level, bringing understanding, inner transformation, and a turning toward God that brings healing to all of life.[6]

INVITATION TO PRESENCE

✿

PRACTICING: MEDITATING ON SCRIPTURE

In the early days of the church, the Christian believers continued to pray and meditate on the scriptures. Peter and the apostles placed such a high priority on their need for prayer and the word that they asked for the appointment of deacons to assist them in the growing ministry needs in Jerusalem. With this extra help they could "devote [themselves] to prayer and to serving the word" (Acts 6:4).

Over time, this spiritual discipline of prayerful listening and meditating on scripture received some structure. The Benedictine communities of the sixth century allowed their life to grow out of this prayerful listening. Called *lectio divina* or "sacred reading," this spiritual discipline assists us in our receptivity as God's spoken word moves from our head to our heart and then into all of our life.

First prepare yourself to be open to listening; open your attention to God. (See chapter 2, pages 23–25.) After an initial prayer for openness to God "who is at work in you" (Philippians 2:13), turn to the text below:

At that time Jesus said, "I thank you, Father, Lord of heaven and earth, because you have hidden these things from the wise and the intelligent and have revealed them to infants; yes, Father, for such was your gracious will. All things have been handed over to me by my Father; and no one knows the Son except the Father, and no one knows the Father except the Son and anyone to whom the Son chooses to reveal him.

"Come to me, all you that are weary and are carrying heavy burdens, and I will give you rest. Take my yoke upon you, and learn from me; for I am gentle and humble in heart, and you will find rest for your souls. For my yoke is easy, and my burden is light."

—Matthew 11:25-30

Read the text, stopping when a word or phrase stands out for you. This awareness may not be a strong one, but when a word or phrase slows your attention down, stay there.

Meditate on the word or phrase. Allow it to sound slowly and gently within you, sinking gradually to deeper levels of your awareness. Allow the word or phrase to enter all the rooms of your life.

Respond to God in prayer about what your discoveries as God uses the word from scripture to read your life.

Be still and simply rest in the spacious and gracious presence of God.

Reflection

❀   How has God's presence surprised you through praying with scripture?

❀   What feelings/attitudes did you carry with you as you began reflecting on the scripture?

❀   What feelings/attitudes do you have now?[7]

❀   What shift or change has occurred in you?

❀   Where is this shift taking you? (toward God, away from God?)

Other scripture to pray during the week. One particular passage or phrase may draw you. If so, stay with that. Do not feel that you must read and meditate on all the passages offered. Receptive and transformational reading is not an attempt to cover as much as possible but an invitation to presence, an openness to God's speaking to the inner heart to bring healing and transformation to all of life.

> Trust in the Lord, and do good;
>   so you will live in the land, and enjoy security.
> Take delight in the Lord,
>   and [God] will give you the desires of your heart. . . .
> Be still before the Lord, and wait patiently for [God];
>   do not fret over those who prosper in their way.
>   —Psalm 37:3-4, 7

> For God alone my soul waits in silence,
>   for my hope is from [God]. . . .
> Trust in [God] at all times, O people;
>   pour out your heart before [God];
> God is a refuge for us.
> Those of low estate are but a breath,
>   those of high estate are a delusion;
> in the balances they go up;
>   they are together lighter than a breath. . . .
>   Steadfast love belongs to you, O Lord.
>   —Psalm 62:5, 8-9, 12

> Ho, everyone who thirsts, come to the waters;
> and you that have no money, come, buy and eat!
> Come, buy wine and milk
>   without money and without price.
> Why do you spend your money
>   for that which is not bread,
>   and your labor for that which does not satisfy?
> Listen carefully to me, and eat what is good. . . .

Incline your ear, and come to me;
   listen so that you may live.

—Isaiah 55:1-3

Do not keep striving for what you are to eat and what you
are to drink, and do not keep worrying. For it is the nations
of the world that strive after all these things, and your Father
knows that you need them. Instead, strive for his kingdom,
and these things will be given to you as well. Do not be
afraid, little flock, for it is your Father's good pleasure to
give you the kingdom. Sell your possessions, and give alms.
Make purses for yourselves that do not wear out, an unfail-
ing treasure in heaven, where no thief comes near and no
moth destroys. For where your treasure is, there your heart
will be also.

—Luke 12:29-34

Consider your own call, brothers and sisters: not many of
you were wise by human standards, not many were powerful, not many were of noble birth. But God chose what is
foolish in the world to shame the wise; God chose what is
weak in the world to shame the strong; God chose what is
low and despised in the world, things that are not, to reduce
to nothing things that are, so that no one might boast in the
presence of God. He is the source of your life in Christ
Jesus, who became for us wisdom from God, and righteousness and sanctification and redemption.

—1 Corinthians 1:26-30

[Jesus] went up the mountain; and after he sat down, his disciples
came to him. Then began to speak, and taught them, saying:
     "Blessed are the poor in spirit, for
theirs is kingdom of God.
     "Blessed are those who mourn,
for they will be comforted.
     "Blessed are the meek, for they will inherit the earth.

"Blessed are those who hunger and thirst for righteousness, for they will be filled.

"Blessed are the merciful, for they will receive mercy.

"Blessed are the pure in heart, for they will see God.

"Blessed are the peacemakers, for they will be called children of God.

"Blessed are those who are persecuted for righteousness' sake, for theirs is the kingdom of heaven.

"Blessed are you when people revile you and persecute you and utter all kinds of evil against you falsely on my account. Rejoice and be glad, for your reward is great in heaven, for in the same way they persecuted the prophets who were before you."

—Matthew 5:1-11

Back on the path

❀

When my children were small, and I had little space for longer times of solitude and prayer, I discovered the *lectio divina* prayer form. The invitation to carry with me throughout the day (and sometimes through the night), the word or phrase that drew my attention was helpful. While folding clothes, washing dishes, doing the routine tasks, I began repeating those few words to myself, allowing them to sink more deeply into my heart and life.

This week, carry the word or phrase with you that has drawn your attention into your life of work and activity. In this way we learn to pray in all of life as a response to God's invitation to presence.

58 ❀ INVITATION TO PRESENCE

ENDNOTES

1. Henri J. M. Nouwen, *Here and Now* (New York: The Crossroad Publishing Co., 1994), 70.

2. Margaret Guenther, *Holy Listening* (Boston, MA: Cowley Publications, 1992), 49. See also J. Reiling and J.L. Swellengrebel, *A Translator's Handbook of the Gospel of Luke* (London: United Bible Societies, 1971), 425–26. Acts 22:3 refers to Paul's learning at the feet of Gamaliel—a common posture for disciples.

3. Teresa of Avila, *Interior Castle*, 231.

4. George Eldon Ladd, *A Commentary on the Revelation of John* (Grand Rapids, MI: William B. Eerdmans Publishing Co., 1972), 68.

5. William S. Plumer, *Psalms* (Carlisle, PA: The Banner of Truth Trust, 1975), 20–21. Although the meaning for *Selah* is not entirely clear, scholars generally agree that it is a musical term inviting the one singing or playing an instrument to "lift up" the tone. This lifting up is also then an invitation to the heart to lift its attention up to God.

6. Jesus refers to this receptive and meditative listening to what God is saying, with the resulting shift of what one understands in the heart, in Matthew 13:14-15, which is a quote from Isaiah 6:9-10. Since Jesus is fully aware that many people do not listen in this way— including ourselves—he asks us to pay attention to how we listen.

7. I am indebted to Tilden Edwards who says that reflection questions help us claim our spiritual experience for ourselves. See also his book *Living in the Presence: Disciplines for the Spiritual Heart* (New York: Harper & Row Publishers, 1987).

FOR FURTHER READING

Hall, Thelma. *Too Deep for Words: Rediscovering Lectio Divina.* Mahwah, NJ: Paulist Press, 1988.

Thelma Hall provides focused and helpful guidance for the practice of meditation on the scriptures.

Miller, Wendy. *Learning to Listen: A Guide for Spiritual Friends.* Nashville, TN: Upper Room Books, 1993.

This book gives guidance for praying the scripture in the Gospel of Matthew.

5

BEING SILENT IN GOD'S PRESENCE

*Talking to God can be an
obstacle to the experience of
God and the divine
intervention in our lives.†*
—Helen and Leonard Doohan

*J*an was in her tenth year of
teaching fifth grade. Happily
married and the mother of
two children, she could not find any
reason for the restlessness she felt. A
good organizer, Jan managed to balance her work with family life and
the family's involvement in a local
congregation.

"I love what I'm doing," she
said. "I couldn't ask for anything
more. I have no reason to feel dissatisfied, but I do."

"Tell me about your dissatisfaction," I invited. "Does it seem to be
with something or someone outside of
yourself or more from within?"

60

Jan sat quietly for a minute or two, and then said, "I can't think of anything outside of myself. It's inside. But the only thing that comes to mind is distance. Distance from God."

"If you were to draw a picture of what that distance looks like, what would you see?" I asked.

After some reflection, Jan said, "I see myself praying, talking. And God listening. But the words are filling up the space between me and God, and I just keep on talking and getting more and more dissatisfied."

"Seems like the words are getting in the way of you and God," I said.

"My talking is creating the distance?"

"Possibly. Have you ever thought that your feelings of dissatisfaction might be God's way of getting your attention?" I asked. "It seems that you have felt confident about coming to God, believing that God listens. But I wonder how much attention you have paid to God."

"Like noticing God?"

"Yes."

"I don't think I've ever done that," Jan said thoughtfully. "Maybe I've been too caught up in my own agenda."

I told Jan about my own experience of concentrating more on what I was praying and whether or not God would answer, than on God. "One winter it began to dawn on me that I hadn't been paying very much attention to God and really didn't know God that well. I knew lots of things about God, and I knew I had a personal faith in Christ, but I had seldom been silent and included God in my awareness."

"Silent? You mean just being silent in prayer?"

"Yes, just being silent and present to God."

❀

Like Jan, many of us think of prayer as addressing God—whether in praise, confession, thanksgiving, or supplication. And for the most part, we expect God to speak to us through scripture, a sermon, or a hymn. Many persons speak of God's communicating through the answers they receive to prayer: "Yes" if God grants the petition and "No" if God does not grant one's request.

However, those moments may come when we are aware of an invitation to be silent, and we open our attention to God. The invitation may come in odd ways; and like Jan, we may not always realize that the One addressing us is God. At times like these, counsel from a wise and prayerful spiritual guide can help. The growing availability of spiritual directors, centers for prayer and spiritual formation, and books on prayer are all a response to the expanding awareness among persons at the end of the twentieth century that we are at heart spiritual, and restless until we find our rest in God.

> Often what draws us to another person . . . for assistance in the spiritual journey is some discontent or dis-ease with our prayer. For some, familiar and dependable methods just aren't working any more; God isn't present in the once familiar ways.[1]

For Jan, a feeling of dissatisfaction led her to notice some distance from God in her prayer experience. Learning to wait in God's presence without words was not easy for her, since she felt as if she were not doing anything or being productive. Dave, a lab technician in the local medical center, found himself both drawn to silence and repelled by it.

"I didn't know what to do," he said. "All kinds of thoughts went around in my head, and once they subsided I tried to figure out what was supposed to happen. Only after a while did it occur to me that I didn't have to make anything happen. I could just rest and wait in God's presence. Then I realized what my problem was: I was letting go of control. No longer did I have control of

God. I began to understand a little more of what it means to call
Jesus Lord. He's in charge!"

When we allow Jesus to direct our attention to the field of
the world, he describes God as the Lord of the harvest (Matthew
9:38). If we are to labor in God's harvest, we need to know the
heart and the ways of the field's owner. We also need to pay attention to how God is at work in the inner field, our heart. That is
also the place for God to be Lord of the harvest. As we are silent
in God's presence, we realize that we not only desire to do the
work of God, we are the work of God.

WALK INTO THE FIELD

❦

LISTENING TO JESUS

Jesus has been telling a story about the seeds' being planted in different kinds of soils: the hard path, the rocky soil, the thorn-infest-
ed soil. Now he continues his story:

> Other seeds fell on good soil and brought forth grain, some
> a hundredfold, some sixty, some thirty. Let anyone with ears
> [to hear] listen!
>
> —Matthew 13:8

Later Jesus explains,

> But as for what was sown on good soil, this is the one who
> hears the word and understands it, who indeed bears fruit
> and yields, in one case a hundredfold, in another sixty, and
> in another thirty.
>
> —Matthew 13:23

Jesus also tells us to hold the word in our hearts, and we will bear
fruit with patient endurance (Luke 8:15). At last the seed sinks

into a soil where it can put down roots and begin to grow. In time the plant yields a harvest. Jesus now shifts his attention to what happens when we not only hear the word he is speaking but in the stillness of our heart pay attention, allowing the good news to put down roots, to find a home in us, and to bear fruit.

DIGGING DEEPER

The roots grow, branching out to the left, to the right, and down, deeper into the soil, drawing in the rich food of the earth and drinking in water. Silently, unseen, the soil and the water give a place to root and life nourishment to the plant. The plant stays still, breathing in the sun and air above the ground, drinking in through its roots below the ground. Being silent in God's presence—simply waiting and resting—assists us to be nourished, to be rooted, and to drink from the inner spring of the Spirit.

The writer once again summons us to the Gospel story. The writer calls us to enter into the heat of the day. It is noon. The disciples have gone to buy food. The townsfolk do not come to the well in the heat of the day. But that is where Jesus chooses to sit. In the silence and solitude a woman comes near, a woman with whom Jews would not socialize because of her gender, race, and reputation. She comes to avoid the crowd but encounters Jesus. Soon, the One who first asks her for a drink is offering her water from the inner spring of the Spirit:

> Those who drink of the water that I will give them will never be thirsty. The water that I will give will become in them a spring of water gushing up to eternal life.
>
> —John 4:14

The woman does not realize that Jesus is speaking about her inner life. She thinks he is talking about some magical water that will quench her thirst and ease her work of hauling buckets each day. In the same way, we appreciate new technologies that save us work, make our life easier. However, Jesus is not a new gadget, and spiritual disciplines are not a new invention designed to get our work done with instant efficiency.

When the woman asks Jesus to give her the water he speaks of, he asks her a question that probes the recesses of her heart. Only then does this thirsty person realize who Jesus really is, and she opens her attention to the One who is present and aware of all that has happened in her unhappy life. To her surprise this Jew, this Messiah, this prophet who knows her life, does not shun her because of multiple marriages or because she lives with a man who is not her husband. Jesus stays and speaks to her of what God is doing and of her inclusion in the Greater Reality of God's gracious kingdom. In her joy, the woman goes back the village and calls the people to come and meet the Messiah, the "man who told me everything I have ever done!" (John 4:29).

God waits for us to notice. In the silence and solitude of the wellspring, God waits for us.

LISTENING WITH OTHERS IN THE FAITH COMMUNITY

. . . in the Hebrew Scriptures

After an exhausting but victorious encounter with the false prophets of Baal, the queen threatens Elijah's life. Elijah's fatigue stems not only from faithful and hard work but also from his tendency to believe that God's work would get done only if he did it. It was all up to him. No others were faithful and true.

Under the strain, Elijah flees into the wilderness and tells God that he wants to die. Instead of answering his request, God leads Elijah deeper into the solitude and silence of the wilderness. Instead of coming in the great wind, an earthquake, or a fire, God comes in the "sound of sheer silence." In the silence Elijah was able to hear God's creative and recreative Word.[2] He knew he was no longer alone; others were also faithful. Elijah knew his life was in God's hands, not in the hands of the queen.

Reflection
When you think about simply being silent in God's presence, what is your inner response?

Others in the Hebrew Scriptures also have prayed in expectant silence. In the midst of the distorted values and stresses of the world, the psalms offer a prayer, guiding us into our waiting on God in silence:

> For God alone my soul waits in silence,
>   for my hope is from [God].
> [God] alone is my rock and my salvation,
>   my fortress; I shall not be shaken.
> On God rests my deliverance and my honor.
>   —Psalm 62:5-7

This is the silence of waiting, listening, trusting. It is the quiet of waiting in hope, even when the world around us is demanding that we listen to its noisy voices and values in order to be someone of value. In the silence before God, we begin to know who we truly are and who gives us value.

Jesus draws our attention to little children and tells us to change and become like children. Only then will we enter the kingdom of heaven. (Read Matthew 18:3.) Psalm 131 provides a short prayer to help us move out of analytical head busyness and into the quiet, simple heart rest of the child.

> O Lord, my heart is not lifted up,
>   my eyes are not raised too high;
> I do not occupy myself with things
>   too great and too marvelous for me.
> But I have calmed and quieted my soul,
>   like a weaned child with its mother;
> my soul is like the weaned child
>   that is with me.

Reflection
Which kind of stillness—that of waiting in expectant silence or that of restful silence—do you sense you need just now?

. . . in the New Testament community
Jesus calls us to make our home in him, in the same way that he makes our home in us:

> I am the true vine, and my Father is the vinegrower. He removes every branch in me that bears no fruit. Every branch that bears fruit he prunes to make it bear more fruit. . . . Abide in me as I abide in you. Just as the branch cannot bear fruit by itself unless it abides in the vine, neither can you unless you abide in me . . . because apart from me you can do nothing. . . . Abide in my love.
> —John 15:1-2, 4, 5, 9

Silence and stillness in God's presence help us stay connected, help us realize who gives us our life and who nourishes the image of Christ and the work of God in us and through us.

INVITATION TO PRESENCE

❀

PRACTICING: BEING SILENT IN GOD'S PRESENCE

Take a few minutes to enter into this time of prayerful presence. Use one of the exercises of coming into God's presence given in chapter 2 if this is helpful to you.

After a prayer of openness to God who is at work in you, turn to one of the passages of scripture below.

> Be still before the Lord, and wait patiently for [God].
> —Psalm 37:7

Be still, and know that I am God!

—Psalm 46:10

Listen to me in silence, . . .
let the people renew their strength.

—Isaiah 41:1

Hear Jesus asking you, "Remain here, and stay awake with me" (Matthew 26:38). Repeat the words to yourself several times, allowing their content and meaning to sink deeply into your heart. Now be still, simply present and open to God. Do not try to make anything happen. Simply wait. Be present.

If thoughts begin to crowd your mind, or feelings begin to bring noise into the silence, bring the scripture you read to mind and repeat it slowly, quietly. Then be silent again.

Gradually increase the time of waiting in silence from ten to twenty minutes.

JOURNALING

Out of silence, respond to God about what you became aware of. Make a note in your journal of your experience of waiting in silence. The following questions may help:

☘ In what way were you aware of God's or Jesus' presence?
☘ How did being silent affect your presence for God? your sense of being in control?
☘ In what way were you aware of being more open to God or known to God?

BACK ON THE PATH

❀

This week allow the verse(s) of scripture you are using to help you enter into silent presence with God, to assist you into quietness during your usual daily work and activity. Touch into that silence, opening your attention to God and simply resting in God's presence for that little time

. . . while waiting at a stoplight,

. . . while standing in line at the supermarket,

. . . before responding in a group discussion,

. . . as you look out of a window or walk outside,

. . . as you take a break between tasks,

. . . before you begin a new task,

. . . while holding a child.

During your longer times of solitude and prayer, make a note in your journal of your experience of silence and presence for God during your daily activity.

ENDNOTES

† Helen and Leonard Doohan, *Prayer in the New Testament: Make Your Requests Known to God* (Collegeville, MN: The Liturgical Press, 1992), 17.

1. Rose Mary Dougherty, "Discernment in Prayer," Shalem News, (June 1990): 8.

2. Henri J. M. Nouwen, *The Way of the Heart: Desert Spirituality and Contemporary Ministry* (New York: HarperCollins, 1991), 58.

FOR FURTHER READING

Keating, Thomas. *Open Mind, Open Heart: The Contemplative Dimension of the Gospel.* New York: Continuum, 1994.

A Cistercian priest residing at St. Benedict's monastery in Snowmass, Colorado, Keating gives a helpful overview of the history of silent contemplative prayer in the Christian tradition, as well as guidance in the practice of this spiritual discipline.

6

ENTERING
THE STORY
IN SCRIPTURE

*Whoever has seen me has
seen the Father.*
—John 14:9

S arah had noticed a change in
how she was reading the
scriptures and praying; the
landscape of her prayer life no
longer looked the same. We arranged
a quiet, uninterrupted time to talk
about what she was experiencing.

"For some months I find I've
been drawn to the Gospels," she
began. "Drawn to the accounts of
Jesus and the disciples, and the people
who came to listen or to be healed.
What's different is how I'm reading.
I'm not sure I would even call it reading any more," Sarah reflected.

"How would you describe it?" I
asked.

For a minute or two Sarah was silent as she paid closer attention to her experience in prayer.

"I'm not quite sure, but I think I was holding the scriptures at a bit of a distance, even though I was reading and following a devotional guide. Now I'm beginning to notice what is happening in the story—as if someone in the Gospel narrative is saying, 'Would you like to join us?' and so you stop and step a little closer. I think my reading has changed to being present with the people in the story. I begin seeing who is there, where Jesus is and what he is doing. Sometimes I just sit in wonder—at what Jesus says and does, like when he was leaving Jericho and stopped to give attention to a blind beggar, right in the middle of the street. Or when he notices a woman in the synagogue with a bent back. And he heals her. . . . I think it's about Jesus' kindness, his noticing people others maybe wouldn't always notice."

"What would happen if Jesus noticed you?" I asked.

Sarah smiled. "I've wondered about that. I think I've been hiding among the crowd."

"What do you think your hiding is about?"

"Well, I know I've always prayed, but I think I'm afraid of meeting God, or Jesus—wondering what God would think of me."

"Do you think it's possible that God is the one who has been inviting you to slow down and notice what is happening in the Gospels and how kind Jesus is?"

"I hadn't thought of that, but it feels right. Maybe God is kinder than I think. I'm beginning to realize that I've been seeing God as someone who is always out to get me if I don't measure up."

Sarah's image of God was beginning to change.

❀

How we see God and what God truly is like are often two different things. However, while we may understand this distinction as a theological or doctrinal truth, our heart has its own habitual ways of seeing—ways that can darken the sense of our understanding when it comes to knowing God. This clouding of our spiritual sight comes from two sources: first, how our false, constricted self sees; second, from abusive experience and/or false teaching. Both distort how we see God, ourselves, and others.

> Many people who desire a closer relationship with God have an image of God that makes closeness difficult. For example, whether it derives from childhood relationships with parents or other authority figures or from the way God was presented . . . an image of God as a demanding, harsh, all-knowing taskmaster cannot sustain a desire for closeness with God.[1]

Rather, such an image creates anxiety. Our driven, frantic lifestyles are often symptomatic of the inner pain and tension we experience because we are not at peace. We maintain some kind of distance from God.

WALK INTO THE FIELD

❀

SEEING WITH JESUS

If we slow down on the path and walk into the field, we will gradually become aware that the persons who knew Jesus have been telling their experience of Jesus in such a way as to draw us into the scene and into our own encounter with Christ.[2]

Luke, one of the Gospel writers, invites us to notice a life-changing event in Nazareth, the village where Jesus lived as a boy. It is the sabbath, and Jesus gathers with the local townsfolk in the synagogue. The moment comes for the reading of the

Hebrew Scriptures, and Jesus receives the scroll of the prophet Isaiah. For a few moments all is quiet as Jesus unrolls the scroll and scans its contents. Then he begins reading, and we notice that he is not just reciting scripture but is drawing our attention toward himself:

> The Spirit of the Lord is upon me,
>   because [the Lord] has anointed me
>   to bring good news to the poor.
> [God] has sent me to proclaim
>   release to the captives
> and recovery of sight to the blind,
>   to let the oppressed go free,
> to proclaim the year of the Lord's favor.
>   —Luke 4:18-19

We begin to realize that healing for our impaired vision—our distorted images of God, our bondage to anxious and driven escape—is at the heart of the gospel and is what Jesus is about. However, healing for our blindness and freedom from captivity is not what we may want to admit we need. Like the people in Nazareth who are faithful in their attendance at the synagogue, we may not see who Jesus really is—and so we avoid what he has to say. Soon after the sabbath gathering, the people drive him out of town and even try to kill him (Luke 4:29). Our resistance to seeing our true condition may be equally violent.

But Jesus does not respond in violence. Instead, he finds direction for his work in the quiet of God's presence in a deserted place. With patience and love, he continues to proclaim the good news of the kingdom of God—a kingdom that is not about abusive domination but healing and freedom (Luke 4:42-44).

Gradually people do listen—people who are not considered good or holy according to the current religious standards gather around Jesus. The religious leaders grumble about the kind of company Jesus keeps and run negative press reports saying, "This fellow welcomes sinners and eats with them" (Luke 15:2). In response to their criticism and in the hearing of those who desire to find a way home to God, Jesus tells a parable:

> There was a man who had two sons. The younger of them said to his father, "Father, give me the share of the property that will belong to me." So he divided his property between them. A few days later the younger son gathered all he had and traveled to a distant country, and there he squandered his property in dissolute living. When he had spent everything, a severe famine took place throughout that country, and he began to be in need. So he went and hired himself out to one of the citizens of that country, who sent him to his fields to feed the pigs. He would gladly have filled himself with the pods that the pigs were eating; and no one gave him anything. But when he came to himself he said, "How many of my father's hired hands have bread enough and to spare, but here I am dying of hunger! I will get up and go to my father, and I will say to him, 'Father, I have sinned against heaven and before you; I am no longer worthy to be called your son; treat me like one of your hired hands.'" So he set off and went to his father. But while he was still far off, his father saw him and was filled with compassion; he ran and put his arms around him and kissed him. Then the son said to him, "Father, I have sinned against heaven and before you; I am no longer worthy to be called your son. Treat me as one of your hired servants." But the father said to his slaves, "Quickly, bring out a robe—the best one—and put it on him; put a ring on his finger and sandals on his feet. And get the fatted calf and kill it, and let us eat and celebrate; for this son of mine was dead and is alive again; he was lost and is found!" And they began to celebrate.
>
> —Luke 15:11-24

DIGGING DEEPER

Jesus helps us see that God is the waiting father; the father who stands on the front porch, scanning the horizon, searching the road, eagerly awaiting our return. Jesus shows us that returning to God is coming home. In God we know who we truly are, and we are at rest.

After spending everything, the younger son in the parable begins to recognize his need. No longer able to live the high life, he slows down and finally comes to himself. His false self is no longer fed, pampered, and given the power to mask what is happening. Hungry and alone, the young man recognizes where home is. However, he does not see himself being welcomed by his father as a son, only as a slave. He will work his way home!

This teaching is that of the religious leaders of the day: keep the law and the traditions, and you will be righteous. This thinking translates into

❦ God is picky and only accepts persons who keep all the commandments.

❦ Since religious leaders represent God, they only approve of persons who are morally and religiously correct and who keep all the commandments and traditions.

❦ We are only "in" with God and the church if we keep all the rules.

Jesus, in contrast, comes bearing good news about God. He spoke his harshest words to those who insisted on laying heavy burdens of rules and laws on the shoulders of people. Jesus named these burden makers "blind leaders of the blind."[3]

In the parable Jesus paints a picture of God as the father who loves us and waits for us to come home, running to meet us with ecstatic joy and compassion—throwing a party in our honor, and celebrating along with the angels in heaven at our homecoming. (See Luke 15:7, 10.) When we talk about being a slave and needing to work our way, God tells us who we are: We are God's children! We belong.

Gradually it dawns on us that we have a place because we are sons and daughters in God's family. We are home. We respond in service to God and one another because of who we are, not because we are trying to earn our way.

Reflection

Imagine that you are returning home to God. What kind of response do you expect?

LISTENING WITH OTHERS IN THE FAITH COMMUNITY

. . . in the Hebrew Scriptures

Familiar with the continent of the heart, the Hebrew believers erected markers here and there as they walked their soul journey. These signposts were names they had given God out of their experience as God's people. Later, when praying—because of their need for renewal of hope and strength or because of their desire to praise and thank Yahweh—these markers served as a place to stop and enter the experience of God and God's goodness once again.

Moses sets up such a marker in the heart's interior as he remembers God's guidance through that howling waste of wilderness between Egypt and Canaan. The Lord had sustained and shielded his people, hovering over them like a mother bird:

> As an eagle stirs up its nest, and hovers over its young;
> as it spreads its wings, takes them up,
>   and bears them aloft on its pinions,
> the Lord alone guided [Israel]. . . .
> [God] set [Israel] atop the heights of the land,
>   and fed [Israel] with produce of the field;
> [the Lord] nursed [Israel] with honey from the crags,
>   with oil from flinty rock;

curds from the herd, and milk from the flock.
—Deuteronomy 32:11-14

Once in the land of Canaan, the people still needed markers to help them remember to turn to God when in need. Their prayer book describes God as a safe place in which to find refuge:

The Lord is my rock, my fortress, and my deliverer,
    my God, my rock in whom I take refuge, . . .
    my stronghold.
—Psalm 18:2

Hebrew Scriptures also picture God as a Creator-Shepherd. We are sheep, the flock of God's pasture:

The Lord is my shepherd, I shall not want.
    He makes me lie down in green pastures;
he leads me beside still waters;
    he restores my soul.
—Psalm 23:1-3

O come, let us worship and bow down,
    let us kneel before the Lord, our Maker!
For he is our God,
    and we are the people of his pasture,
    and the sheep of his hand.
—Psalm 95:6-7

Reflection
Take a few minutes now, and notice which image of God draws you as you reflect on these Hebrew Scriptures. What kinds of God-markers are you aware of in your own experience?

.... in the New Testament community

The disciples are slow to see what Jesus is trying to show them about God. They struggle with denial, fear, and a host of questions as Jesus prepares them for his death, resurrection, and his departure. In the intimate conversation following their observance of the Passover meal, Jesus explains that one day they will come to be with him. They will come to God because they know Jesus. He explains, "If you know me, you will know my Father also. From now on you do know him and have seen him" (John 14:7).

Seen God? His words surprise them. Suddenly their images of God and the teaching about God in their tradition collide. They are Jews and know the accounts of those who have encountered God and feared for their life. Moses saw the burning bush but hid his face as soon as he realized Who was present, "for he was afraid to look at God" (Exodus 3:6). Later Moses is told that he cannot see God's face and live (33:20). But even so, deep within the disciples' hearts lay the desire to see God. They are familiar with Job and the complaint he filed concerning God's absence:

> Oh, that I knew where I might find him,
> that I might come even to his dwelling!
> I would lay my case before him,
> and fill my mouth with arguments.
> I would learn what he would answer me. . . .
> If I go forward, his is not there;
> or backward, I cannot perceive him;
> on the left he hides, and I cannot behold him.
> —Job 23:3-5, 8-9

Now Jesus is saying they have seen God. Where? When? Philip voices the statement they all are thinking, "Lord, show us the Father, and we will be satisfied." Jesus replies, "Have I been with you all this time, Philip, and you still do not know me? Whoever has seen me has seen the Father" (John 14:8-9).

Although the truth sits before them—they are seeing the One who has been unseen (Colossians 1:15)—the disciples are unsure. Their belief system still informs their vision, clouding their heart's understanding of who Jesus truly is. Jesus speaks to their unbelief, instructing them on what to notice: "Pay attention to what I say and what I do. Look at what I do, and you will see God. The Father who dwells in me does the works" (John 14:10-11, author's paraphrase).

The spiritual discipline of entering the story in scripture assists us to open our attention and to see more clearly who Jesus is and what God is like.

Reflection
Imagine yourself in the upper room with the disciples as Jesus tells them: "Whoever has seen me has seen the Father." Reflect on your response.

. . . . in the early church and beyond
Following Pentecost and the coming of the Holy Spirit, the followers of Christ become aware of the presence of the risen Jesus among them and in them. They acknowledge the reality of Jesus' words in their experience: "Remember, I am with you always, to the end of the age" (Matthew 28:20). Jesus also told them:

> I will ask the Father, and he will give you another Advocate, to be with you forever. This is the Spirit of truth, whom the world cannot receive, because it neither sees him nor knows him. You know him, because he abides with you, and he will be in you.
>
> —John 14:16-17

The disciples announce their experience to others, and if we listen in on their conversations with persons they meet as they spread the good news throughout the Greek, Roman, Egyptian, African world, we will hear them saying,

We declare to you what was from the beginning, what we
have heard, what we have seen with our eyes, what we have
looked at and touched with our hands, concerning the word
of life—this life was revealed, and we have seen it and tes-
tify to it, and declare to you the eternal life that was with the
Father and was revealed to us—we declare to you what we
have seen and heard so that you also may have fellowship
with us; and truly our fellowship is with the Father and with
his Son Jesus Christ.

—1 John 1:1-3

The disciples' writing and speech invite us to encounter Jesus and
to allow Jesus to encounter us.

In the early Middle Ages, the invitation to walk into the
scripture story and encounter Jesus often came through the publi-
cation of illustrated versions of the Gospels. Numerous pen-draw-
ings accompanied the Gospel accounts (for many persons could
not read). They depicted Jesus among the people he taught,
healed, welcomed, and told stories to. These pictorial Gospels
included instructions to help the reader slow down and begin to
notice who was present in the Gospel story and what was happening. The pictures and instructions invite the reader to enter the
story, to be present and participate in the event, and to be present
to Jesus.

Church tradition credits Bonaventure (1217–74), a Fran-
ciscan and Doctor of the Church, with the preparation of one of
the more well-known editions of an illustrated Gospel and prayer
guide.[4] The Franciscans preached the gospel, cared for the poor,
and received empowerment for living and ministry from a deep
and vibrant life of prayer and biblical meditation. The illustrated
Gospel and prayer guide helped laypersons know and enter into
the Gospel narrative. Ignatius of Loyola, founder of the Society of
Jesus (Jesuits) in the sixteenth century, also came to personal faith
in Christ as he entered the Gospel stories during a painful and
long convalescence following surgery. Profoundly moved and

transformed by his experience, Ignatius prepared a series of guided meditations that helped persons enter the scripture and be in Jesus' presence.

In his book, *Celebration of Discipline*, Quaker writer Richard Foster refers to this entering of the scripture story as meditating on the scriptures. He writes,

> Seek to live the experience, remembering the encouragement of Ignatius of Loyola to apply all our senses to our task. Smell the sea. Hear the lap of water along the shore. See the crowd. Feel the sun on your head and the hunger in your stomach. Taste the salt in the air. Touch the hem of his garment. In this regard Alexander Whyte counsels us, ". . . the truly Christian imagination never lets Jesus Christ out of her sight. . . . You open your New Testament. . . . And, by your imagination, that moment you are one of Christ's disciples on the spot, and are at His feet." . . . Always remember that we enter the story not as passive observers, but as active participants. Also remember that Christ is truly with us to teach us, to heal us, to forgive us.[5]

INVITATION TO PRESENCE

✿

PRACTICING: ENTERING THE STORY IN SCRIPTURE

First take a few minutes to slow down, to open your attention to God in prayer. Now enter the story in scripture by taking the following steps:

Read Mark 10:46-52 several times:

> As [Jesus] and his disciples and a large crowd were leaving Jericho, Bartimaeus son of Timaeus, a blind beggar, was sitting by the roadside. When he heard that it was Jesus of

Nazareth, he began to shout out and say, "Jesus, Son of
David, have mercy on me!" Many sternly ordered him to be
quiet, but he cried out even more loudly, "Son of David,
have mercy on me!" Jesus stood still and said, "Call him
here." And they called the blind man, saying to him, "Take
heart; get up, he is calling you." So throwing off his cloak,
he sprang up and came to Jesus. Then Jesus said to him,
"What do you want me to do for you?" The blind man said
to him, "My teacher, let me see again." Jesus said to him,
"Go; your faith has made you well." Immediately he
regained his sight and followed him on the way.

Close your eyes and imagine yourself on the road that leaves the
city of Jericho. Visualize the city gate behind you, the sun shining
on the dusty road. Notice who is present: the crowd, walking on
the road alongside Jesus and the disciples; the persons, sitting
alongside the road. Notice the colors, the sounds of voices, the
feel of the dirt road beneath your feet. Now you hear Bartimaeus
shouting, trying to get Jesus' attention.

How do you feel about being present with Jesus and his disciples as the shouting begins? Do you feel embarrassed? uncomfortable? interested? angry? compassionate?

Jesus stops to listen, and then invites the blind beggar to
come to him. Watch as Bartimaeus gets up and makes his way
toward the sound of Jesus' voice. Listen as Jesus asks this man
what he wants. Jesus empowers this powerless man to ask for his
sight, and Jesus gives him what he asks.

Now Jesus turns toward you and asks, "What do you want
me to do for you?" How do you respond?

Take some time to be with Jesus now, either in dialogue or
simple presence.

JOURNALING

Write a few sentences in your journal describing your prayer experience.

Other scripture passages you may use during the week include the following: Matthew 8:1-3; John 1:35-39; Matthew 8:23-27; John 21:1-12.

BACK ON THE PATH

☘

Short prayers can help us open our awareness to God, who is present with us at all times. This week carry this prayer with you on the road: *Lord Jesus, help me to see as you see.*

ENDNOTES

1. William A. Barry, *Seek My Face: Prayer as Personal Relationship in Scripture* (New York: Paulist Press, 1989), 4.
2. Through their use of the historical present tense in the Greek language, Greek authors created a sense of being present, transporting the reader—or the listener—into the actual scene at the time of the occurrence. See "Explanation of General Format," *New American Standard Bible*. Carol Stream, IL: Creation House, 1972. x. Also G. L. Phillips , "Faith and Vision in the Fourth Gospel," *Studies in the Fourth Gospel*, ed. F. L. Cross (London: A. R. Mowbray, 1957), 83–96, quoted in "Appendix I," *The Anchor Bible: The Gospel According to John* (i–xii), 502–503. John uses five different words to express the word *sight*, or "to see." One of these, *theasthai*, can be translated as "contemplate," which according to Phillips means "to look at some dramatic spectacle and in a measure to become a part of it." In his epistle John progresses from *horon* (sight accompanied with real understanding) to *theasthai* (to contemplate and participate

in) when he writes, "Something we have seen (*horan*) with our own eyes, something we have actually looked at (*theasthai*)" (1 John 1:1).

3. Here Jesus makes direct reference to the spiritual blindness of the religious leaders of his day.

4. Rosalie B. Green and Isa Ragusa, eds., *Meditations on the Life of Christ: An Illustrated Manuscript of the Fourteenth Century* (NJ: Princeton University Press, 1961). These meditations were written to enable the reader to "give heed to understand everything that was said and done, as though you had been present" in the Gospel narrative.

5. Richard J. Foster, *Celebration of Discipline: The Path to Spiritual Growth* (San Francisco, CA: HarperSanFrancisco, 1988), 29–30. Alexander Whyte is a Scottish preacher and the author of *Lord, Teach Us to Pray.* (New York: Harper & Brothers, n.d.). While the scriptures warn us against "vain" (or empty) and evil imagination (which serve no purpose or lead to evil intent and action), the imagination is a gift of God to be enjoyed and used for good. Throughout the scriptures, we discover how the gift of the imagination becomes a servant of the spirit of God and leads us to God.

FOR FURTHER READING

Barry, William A. *Paying Attention to God: Discernment in Prayer.* Notre Dame, IN: Ave Maria Press, 1990. See chapter 9: "What Is God Really Like?"

————. *Seek My Face: Prayer as Personal Relationship in Scripture.* New York: Paulist Press, 1989. See chapter 1: "Our Ambivalence about God" and chapter 12: "Getting to Know Jesus."

Foster, Richard J. *Celebration of Discipline: The Path to Spiritual Growth.* San Francisco, CA: HarperSanFrancisco, 1988. See chapter 2: "Meditation."

7

BRINGING THE WORLD INTO OUR PRAYER

*The Spirit helps us in our weakness; for
we do not know how
to pray as we ought.*
—Romans 8:26

*D*uring the Lenten season,
Roger attended a prayer
retreat. His pastor wanted
to assist persons in the congregation
to deepen their relationship with
God. Although Roger felt a little
apprehensive about spending a
whole day focusing on prayer, he
decided to go.

Julie, one of his granddaugh-
ters, was about to be baptized and
join the church, and her parents had
invited the extended family to attend.
Roger knew he was anxious about
participating. For one thing, his former wife would be there, and then
there was James, Julie's dad and

Roger's son. They had not been as close since the divorce. But at the same time, Roger knew that something good was happening in the lives of James and Debbie and their children.

Roger's pastor had said that Lent was a good time for reflection and change. Roger wondered if a day of quiet and prayer could help him cope with some of the anxiety and stress he felt.

During one of the sessions, the retreat leader invited the participants to enter the Gospel narrative and to open their attention to Jesus and the persons in the story. The story given was one of Jesus' walking up the mountain near the sea of Galilee and the crowds coming to him there, bringing with them the lame, the maimed, the blind, and others who needed healing. Jesus cured them, and the crowd expressed amazement and praised God.

Later, during the small-group sharing time, Roger spoke about what he had noticed as he prayed. "First I came to Jesus for help and healing for myself. But then I noticed my family standing there, and after some time I brought them one by one to Jesus for healing. What struck me was how kind Jesus was to each of us. I don't know how, but his love seemed to melt a lot of my anxiety, and I'm more at peace about being with my family at Julie's baptism. Maybe he's asking me to reach out. I don't know. I know Jesus wants me to show kindness in some way.

❃

Anxiety and fear can kidnap us out of the reality of God's care and presence in difficult situations. Like Roger, we can become tense and distant when past memories and events loom like dark shadows on the horizon of our inner continent of memory and experience. And, as the children of Israel became fearful of freedom in the land before them, so we also can hold back because of the "giants" before us. (Read Numbers 13:1-3, 27-28, 32-33.)

However, Jesus brings us healing and courage. As we spend time in his presence we begin to see differently. He heals our blindness, and we find ourselves moved to pray for ourselves and others in ways we would not have thought possible. This healing is pervasive and enlarges our vision of the world around us.

WALK INTO THE FIELD

✿

SEEING WITH JESUS

In the rhythm of his life, Jesus periodically walks away from the towns and villages into the quiet solitude of the hills to pray. Sometimes he is alone; other times he invites the disciples into retreat with him.

Luke 11 invites us to leave the path of our everyday work and to be in retreat with Jesus and the disciples. Here there is no crowd, no demands. Gradually the tight grip of the world's system begins to loosen, and we become aware of our need for help in the face of need, anger, and fear. We know that Jesus comes into retreat to rest and pray. What can we learn from him? One of the disciples speaks our question for us: "Lord, teach us to pray." Now our time apart in the hills becomes a retreat for prayer. First Jesus gives us a prayer to pray:

When you pray, say:
"Father, hallowed be your name.
  Your kingdom come.
  Give us each day our daily
    bread.
And forgive us our sins,
  for we ourselves forgive

everyone who is indebted to us.
And do not bring us to the
time of trial.

—Luke 11: 1-4

Then Jesus tells a story. He weaves a tale with one of us as the main character, placing us in an embarrassing situation with an empty pantry and unable to fulfill the sacred obligation of hospitality:

Suppose one of you has a friend, and you go to him at midnight and say to him, "Friend, lend me three loaves of bread; for a friend of mine has arrived, and I have nothing to set before him." And he answers from within, "Do not bother me; the door has already been locked, and my children are with me in bed; I cannot get up and give you anything." I tell you, even though he will not get up and give him anything because he is his friend, at least because of his persistence he will get up and give him whatever he needs.

—Luke 11: 5-8

Now Jesus sets commentary alongside the story:

So I say to you, Ask, and it will be given you; search and you will find; knock, and the door will be opened for you. For everyone who asks receives, and everyone who searches finds, and for everyone who knocks, the door will be opened. Is there anyone among you who, if your child asks for a fish, will you give a snake instead of a fish? Or if the child asks for an egg, will give a scorpion? If you then, who are evil, know how to give good gifts to your children, how much more will the heavenly Father give the Holy Spirit to those who ask him!

—Luke 11: 9-13

DIGGING DEEPER

Jesus' prayer is short (only forty words long) and simple enough to remember. It begins by relocating our awareness as to who God is, and therefore who we are. We are children who are safe in the care of our heavenly Parent. As we pray this prayer, God's desire for the kingdom of heaven to come in this world becomes our desire, and we become aware of what the kingdom looks like when it comes. We acknowledge our dependence on God and realize our true needs: daily bread, forgiveness for sins, peace with our neighbor, and protection from trial. And we, in turn, let go of our need to hold grudges and keep long accounts against others. In the way God forgives, we forgive.

This kind of worldview bumps up against the materialistic worldview "which has penetrated deeply into our culture, [causing] many to ignore the spiritual dimensions of life and the spiritual resources of faith."[1] Spiritual disciplines assist us to notice our unbelief and to open our attention to a loving God who spoke all creation into being and who sustains our life. For us to realize our dependence on God, Jesus tells the story of our being caught in need; we become the man who knocks at midnight.

> Travellers often journeyed late in the evening to avoid the heat of the midday sun. In Jesus' story just such a traveller had arrived towards midnight at his friend's house. In the east hospitality is a sacred duty; it was not enough to set before a man bare sufficiency; the guest had to be confronted with an ample abundance. . . .The late arrival of the traveller confronted the householder with an embarrassing situation, because his larder was empty.[2]

With empty hands, we go knocking at the door of our neighbor, knowing that he is in bed and has locked his door for the night.

Just so, our need catapults us into the realm of the Spirit, the presence of God. In order to open a window for us to see what happens when we pray, Jesus sets a commentary alongside the parable. He tells us that when we pray, Someone listens, notices, and responds. God is not just a good neighbor; God is a kind and responsive Parent. Everyone who asks receives; everyone who searches finds; and everyone who comes knocking at the door has the door opened to them. This loving God is waiting and ready, active as we pray.

Jesus' commentary takes a turn at the end. Barclay says it well:

> If a churlish and unwilling householder can in the end be coerced by a friend's shameless persistence into giving him what he needs, how much more will God who is a loving Father supply all his children's needs? "If you," he says, "who are evil, know that you are bound to supply your children's needs, how much more will God?"[3]

Jesus began this time apart of learning to pray by teaching us a prayer to pray. He ends his commentary by instructing us what to ask for, reassuring us that God will give us what we ask. Jesus points to our deepest need, the presence of God within and among us through the presence of the Holy Spirit, for at the core we are spiritual beings. When we come to God, asking for things, Jesus lifts our gaze to see that God is offering us relationship—God's self in the Holy Spirit.

Reflection
In what ways are you aware of your need for God? of your dependence on God?

LISTENING WITH OTHERS IN THE FAITH COMMUNITY

... in the Hebrew Scriptures
In the world of the Old Testament we discover persons who live and pray within the reality of Genesis 1 where the "origin of the things in the world is God, not a random play of physics and

chemistry."[4] They live and pray in response to God who has come to them, restoring broken relationships. (Read Isaiah 43:1.) As we listen to how they pray, we notice that

> the formality and reticence of ecclesiastical prayer is utterly foreign to the Bible. Biblical prayer is impertinent, persistent, shameless, indecorous. It is more like haggling in an outdoor bazaar than the polite monologues of the churches.[5]

In prayer the Hebrews complain, shout, debate, and petition God who is their Creator and Sustainer. We hear Abraham's bargaining with God about the celestial inquiry and plans for destruction of Sodom (Genesis 18:17, 20-23ff.).

After the exodus from slavery in Egypt, the people of Israel become depressed and begin weeping about the daily menu of manna. Moses sounds off at God:

> Did I conceive all this people? Did I give birth to them, that you should say to me, "Carry them in your bosom, as a nurse carries a sucking child," to the land that you promised on oath to their ancestors? . . . I am not able to carry all this people alone, for they are too heavy for me.
>
> —Numbers 11:12, 14

But when the people refuse to enter the promised land and turn against Moses and the other leaders and are about to kill them, Moses intercedes for the people in the face of God's anger:

> Now if you kill this people . . . then the nations who have heard about you will say, "It is because the Lord was not able to bring this people into the land he swore to give them . . . ." And now, therefore, let the power of the Lord be great in the way that you promised when you spoke, saying,
> > "The Lord is slow to anger,
> > and abounding in steadfast love,
> > forgiving iniquity and transgression. . . ."

Then the Lord said, "I do forgive, just as you have asked."
—Numbers 14:15-18, 20

We hear Samuel's consolation of the Israelites as they come to him asking for prayer.

And Samuel said to the people, "Do not be afraid; you have done all this evil, yet do not turn aside from following the Lord, but serve the Lord with all your heart; . . . For the Lord will not cast away his people, for his great name's sake. . . . Moreover as for me, far be it from me that I should sin against the Lord by ceasing to pray for you."
—1 Samuel 12:20, 22, 23

We discover the openness of these people as they pray out of the depths of their despair and anxiety, their boldness as they confront God on behalf of the people, and their great love for God and for the people in their prayers.

Reflection
How open to God am I in my prayers? What longings have I yet to bring into God's presence?

. . . in the New Testament community
If we pause to listen to the prayers of persons in the New Testament community, we become aware that they "live an amphibious life of sense and spirit" and "respond to a world filled with the presence of God and the risen Christ."[6] They pray both in community and in solitude, often following the Jewish pattern of praying three times daily. (See Acts 1:14; 2:42; 3:1; 9:11; 10:9; 12:5.)

Luke invites us to join Peter and John as they pray with other friends after their release from arrest. From Jesus, they have learned to pray in need and in weakness:

Sovereign Lord, who made the heaven and the earth, the sea, and everything in them. . . . in this city . . . both Herod and Pontius Pilate, with the Gentiles and the peoples of Israel, gathered together against your holy servant Jesus, whom you anointed. . . . And now, Lord, look at their threats, and grant to your servants to speak your word with all boldness, while you stretch out your hand to heal, and signs and wonders are performed through the name of your holy servant Jesus.

—Acts 4:24, 27, 29-30

In the face of anxiety, trouble, hostility, and imprisonment, Paul writes to the believers in Philippi about how to find peace through prayer. The New Testament shares his letter with us:

The Lord is near. Do not worry about anything, but in everything by prayer and supplication with thanksgiving let your requests be made known to God. And the peace of God, which surpasses all understanding, will guard your hearts and your minds in Christ Jesus.

—Philippians 4:5-7

These early believers know anxiety, suffering, and trouble. They know the feeling of weakness and terror·that fear brings. In the midst of their weakness, Paul invites them to open their attention to God who is present through the Holy Spirit.

In this movement of turning to God in the midst of need and weakness, the Holy Spirit is present to help us as we pray. Rather than being orphans abandoned to the storms and chaos of this present age, the Holy Spirit reminds us that we are children of God as we cry "Abba! Father!" (Romans 8:15). In the midst of trouble we groan—for ourselves and for others—and the Spirit "helps us in our weakness; for we do not know how to pray as we ought, but that very Spirit intercedes with sighs too deep for words. And God, who searches the heart, knows what is the mind of the Spirit, because the Spirit intercedes for the saints according to the will of God" (Romans 8:26-27).

. . . in the church today

The church is experiencing a widespread renewal of interest in prayer. At a time when churches no longer offer midweek prayer meetings, people everywhere are wanting to learn how to pray.[7] The Holy Spirit seems to be drawing us into a fresh awareness of our need for God. Sometimes we become aware of our spiritual thirst in a quiet, ongoing way; at other times we may feel overwhelmed as we see the center of our political and social structures falling apart. Walter Wink notes that

> this groaning of the Spirit within us is related to the groaning of the created order, subjected, as it is, to futility (Romans 8:20). We are inundated by the cries of an entire creation: the millions now starving to death each year, the tortured, the victims of sexual abuse or battering, the ill.
>
> But that is not all; we also bear inexpressible sorrow for all the . . . plants and trees and fish dying of pollution. . . . We are so interconnected with all of life that we cannot help being touched by the pain of all that suffers. . . . until we risk being crushed by the enormity of it all.[8]

Rather than avoiding the tragic reality in front of us and numbing our awareness in some kind of drugged existence, we receive the invitation to notice what is happening. We realize we do not have to carry it alone. The Holy Spirit helps us in our weakness. We need to pause and become aware that the spirit of Christ within us, who is already praying, prompts any desire on our part to turn toward God in prayer. We do not need to call on God to be present. Rather, we need to open our attention to the spirit of God, which is already present, and notice what God is praying in us.

A spiritual discipline that can assist us in opening our attention to God's presence and God's desires for the needs of the world is to enter the Gospel story with our needs and the needs of others. We bring our needs, the needs of others, and the needs of the world into the presence of Jesus, God in the Son. Then we wait and notice Jesus' response.

While prayer is not a substitute for action, action without prayer has no grounding in God, who is the wellspring of the Spirit of life. Like Roger, as we wait in the presence of Jesus, we become aware of what God is asking of us. We find ourselves freed "from the paralysis that results from being overwhelmed by the immensity of the world's need and our relative powerlessness."9

INVITATION TO PRESENCE

✿

PRACTICING: BRINGING THE WORLD INTO OUR PRAYER

Take a few minutes to enter into this time of prayerful presence. Appreciate the need of time for transition as you open your attention to God. Use one of the preparatory exercises that is helpful to you. Now prepare to bring your needs and the needs of others in the world by entering the following story in scripture.

Read Matthew 9:35-38.

Then Jesus went about all the cities and villages, teaching in their synagogues, and proclaiming the good news of the kingdom, and curing every disease and every sickness. When he saw the crowds, he had compassion for them, because they were harassed and helpless, like sheep without a shepherd. Then he said to his disciples, "The harvest is plentiful, but the laborers are few; therefore ask the Lord of the harvest to send out laborers into his harvest."

Now close your eyes and see yourself following Jesus into the cities and the villages. Notice what city or village you are in and what the people are like. What do you see and smell? What sounds do you hear?

Now Jesus finds the gathering places where people meet to worship, and there he proclaims the good news of the kingdom. He also heals all who are diseased or sick. Where do you find yourself in the meeting place? What is your response as Jesus speaks? as Jesus heals?

Who do you want to bring to Jesus to hear the good news and to receive healing? Join the group of people who are coming to Jesus for healing. Join those who bring others for him to lay hands on and pray.

As you come, bringing your friend(s), family member(s), or other persons in need, wait in Jesus' presence. Watch what he does, and listen to what he says. Respond as you are ready and as needed.

After the meeting, you leave with Jesus and watch as he stands on the busy corner of the city and sees the crowds walking by. You become aware of Jesus' compassion for the people on the street; you find yourself attuned to their sense of harassment and helplessness as they rush to and fro with no one to protect them and guide them to God. How do you feel? What is your response to the crowds?

Now Jesus turns to you and tells you what to pray: "The harvest is plentiful, but the laborers are few; therefore ask the Lord of the harvest to send out laborers into his harvest." What is your prayer now?

JOURNALING

Write a few sentences in your journal to catch your prayer experience.

BACK ON THE PATH

❀

Return to Matthew 9:35-38 or use another passage of scripture if it draws you in some way. Spend time in the various parts of the story. Notice who or what you bring to Jesus, and what response Jesus gives—to them and/or to you. Pay attention also to your own response.

This week carry this prayer with you on the road: *Lord Jesus, help me to see the world as you see it.*

ENDNOTES

1. Walter Wink, "Our Stories, Cosmic Stories, and the Biblical Story," in *Sacred Stories: A Celebration of the Power of Story to Transform and Heal,* eds. Charles Simpkinson and Anne Simpkinson (San Francisco: HarperSanFrancisco, 1993), 211.
2. William Barclay. *The Daily Study Bible Series: The Gospel of Luke,* rev. ed. Philadelphia, PA: The Westminster Press, 1975), 145.
3. Ibid., 146.
4. Bonnie Thurston. *Spiritual Life in the Early Church: The Witness of Acts and Ephesians* (Minneapolis, MN: Fortress Press, 1993), 2–3.
5. Walter Wink. "Prayer and the Powers: History Belongs to the Intercessors," *Sojourners* (October 1990): 13.
6. Thurston, *Spiritual Life in the Early Church,* 3.
7. Marlene Kropf and Eddy Hall, *Praying with the Anabaptists: The Secret of Bearing Fruit* (Newton, KS: Faith and Life Press, 1994), 7.
8. Walter Wink, "God Is the Intercessor: Christians Give Words to the Spirit's Longings," *Sojourners* (November 1990): 23.
9. Ibid., 24.

FOR FURTHER READING

Barry, William A., *God and You: Praying as a Personal Relationship*. New York: Paulist Press, 1988. See chapter 6: "Imagination and Prayer."

Doohan, Helen and Leonard. *Prayer in the New Testament: Make Your Requests Known to God*. Collegeville, MN: The Liturgical Press, 1992.

Koenig, John. *Rediscovering New Testament Prayer: Boldness and Blessing in the Name of Jesus*. San Francisco: HarperSanFrancisco, 1992.

8

SEEING GOD'S CARE IN CREATION

*The earth, O Lord, is full
of your steadfast love.*
—Psalm 119:64

*P*hil was sharing his experience of God. "One of the
ways I become aware of
God is when I'm outside. I remember
being in Gainesville, Florida, at
Bivens Arm Nature Park—a swampy
nature preserve close to where we
lived. I used to go there about once a
month and spend several hours by
myself, walking the trails, sitting on
a bench observing nature, writing in
my journal, reading a book, etc. The
pace of life was fast, both at home
and at the church I pastored. The
loads sometimes seemed heavy, so
this was a place of retreat in which I
found much solace.*

On this one occasion, I observed two remarkable events. As I sat very still about three feet away from a large rock, a small lizard crawled up on it and proceeded to shed its skin—a once-a-year ritual for lizards, I presume. It performed the whole five- to ten-minute procedure in my presence, using its claws to pull off its skin, turning it inside out from the tip of its nose to the end of its tail. I sat transfixed, amazed at God's design in creation.

The second event took place out in the swamp, where a large and graceful bird called a great white egret stood. That sight alone was awe-inspiring enough. But as I watched, I saw it stalk, catch, kill, and finally swallow whole a Florida water rat. Again, I was awestruck by this animal behavior that exhibited not only God's power to create but to sustain.

What I gained from this encounter with nature, and during some other encounters as well, was a deep awareness of God's presence and activity in the world. It brought a refreshing perspective to my harried and hurried life. It brought a realization that God, as both Creator and Sustainer, is interested in the well-being of God's creatures—whether great or small. The care and worries of my life that took place a few miles away in an asphalt jungle, in the context of human institutions, somehow seemed to take on a different light, when I was reminded of the loving and nurturing presence of the Creator God." [1]

WALK INTO THE FIELD

❀

SEEING WITH JESUS

Luke invites us to mingle with the crowd as Jesus speaks about worry. Suddenly a squabble breaks out between two men. It turns out they are brothers. One accuses the other of not giving him his fair share of the family estate. Then he turns toward Jesus and orders him to take on the role of judge, arbitrating a settlement. Jesus hears but does not satisfy the demand. Instead he addresses both men as he exposes the inner continent of their heart condition and stakes a warning sign there: "Watch out and guard yourselves from every kind of greed; because a person's true life is not made up of the things he owns, no matter how rich he may be" (Luke 12:15, TEV).

Then, as they stop fighting long enough to notice the caution sign, Jesus tells a story:

> There was once a rich man who had land which bore good crops. He began to think to himself, "I don't have a place to keep all my crops. What can I do? This is what I will do," he told himself; "I will tear down my barns and build bigger ones, where I will store the grain and all my other goods. Then I will say to myself, Lucky man! You have all the good things you need for many years. Take life easy, eat, drink, and enjoy yourself!" But God said to him, "You fool! This very night you will have to give up your life; then who will get all these things you have kept for yourself?
>
> And Jesus concluded, "This is how it is with those who pile up riches for themselves but are not rich in God's sight."
> —Luke 12:16-21

Then Jesus turns to his disciples. He doesn't tell a parable now. Instead Luke invites us to listen as Jesus exposes the worry factor that hangs like a thick fog over the continent of the inner self, blinding us all to what really matters.

> And so I tell you not to worry about the food you need to stay alive or about the clothes you need for your body. Life is much more important than food, and the body much more important than clothes.

Then he gives a spiritual discipline to practice, an invitation to presence:

> Look at the crows: they don't plant seeds or gather a harvest; they don't have storage rooms or barns; God feeds them! . . . Look how the wild flowers grow: they don't work or make clothes for themselves. But I tell you that not even King Solomon with all his wealth had clothes as beautiful as one of these flowers. It is God who clothes the wild grass—grass that is here today and gone tomorrow. . . . Won't [God] be all the more sure to clothe you? What little faith you have!
>
> So don't be all upset, always concerned about what you will eat and drink. (For the pagans of this world are always concerned about all these things.) Your Father knows that you need these things. Instead, be concerned with his Kingdom, and he will provide you with these things.
>
> —Luke 12:21-31, TEV

DIGGING DEEPER

Jesus tells us we are in danger when the bottom line dominates our decisions and when what we own dictates who we are. Why? Because like the farmer, we do not reckon with God and do not see ourselves for who we really are.[2] The rich landowner sees himself as a lucky man because he has a bumper crop and can now enjoy the good life: he can take it easy; eat, drink, and be happy! However, God sees him differently and calls him a fool. Why? Jesus says it is because he forgets who he is, a person created in the image of God and cared for by God. Creation and a good harvest are not just commodities for our use—to be cut, stored, gloated over, and consumed. They are gifts, given and sustained by God, to enjoy and to share with others. God's goodness is in creation.

When we lose sight of God, we behave as orphans alone in a universe of undetermined origin and unsure future. In our anxiety we either become driven by greed to have more—with no regard to our real needs or the needs of others,[3] or worry snags us—always afraid we will not have enough. "Wealth can represent a danger to those who do not have it as well as to those who do. Jesus emphasizes the importance of trust in God and detachment from things."[4]

This detachment is not a denial of creation, or a false distancing from the earth or our bodies. The detachment Jesus speaks of is a loosening of our clenched fists—no longer holding on to material goods because of greed or worry. The detachment Jesus invites us to is a realization that we are cared for by a loving God who holds us dear and provides us with everything we need.

To make this shift from greed to letting go, from worry to trust, from thinking we are alone in the universe to knowing that a caring God holds us, Jesus invites us to go outside. "Look," he says, "at the birds. Look at the wild flowers."

The word *look* does not mean a casual glance. Nor does it mean seeing what is there and simply naming and categorizing what we notice. This kind of seeing functions according to the rules of an old science that tells us that we can measure and know everything: "All we need to do is perfect our instruments and our methods, and we can collect enough data like birds on a string to predict physical events from physical causes."[5] Physicists today sound more like mystics than scientists as they contemplate the mystery at the heart of the atom. No longer able to "predict the career of any one particle,"[6] the news from the science lab includes such terms as Werner Heisenberg's "a higher power, not influenced by our wishes, which finally decides and judges."[7]

Jesus invites us to contemplate creation. The word *look* (or *consider* in other translations) in Luke's Gospel is really an invitation "to immerse" ourselves in what we see in creation.[8] This kind of perceptive and patient gazing at the birds and wild flowers becomes a window for presence. "Birds and flowers become resonant images for a reality which transcends them" and "evoke an awareness of God's pervasive care and provision."[9] Then the fog of greed and worry disappears in the warm light of the Spirit.

LISTENING WITH OTHERS IN THE FAITH COMMUNITY

. . . in the Hebrew Scriptures

The opening words of the Hebrew Scriptures help us realize that we live in the presence of God: "In the beginning when God created the heavens and the earth . . ." (Genesis 1:1). The God who creates, who speaks all creation into being, also pauses now and then to look at what is and sees that everything that has been made is very good (Genesis 1:31), including humankind—male and female—created in God's image (1:27). God has made all creation in preparation for us and invites us to care for the gift of creation. Death, pain, and back-breaking toil enter the fiber of human life and all the created order only when the first man and woman believe the serpent's lie that God is withholding something from them. (Read Genesis 3.) Yet the pages of Hebrew Scriptures reveal to us that these people know the God who sustains all that is, and that creation is a gift from God.

God calls the family of Israel and chooses the Hebrews to be a witness to God's presence and faithfulness to the world. The Book of Leviticus reminds these former slaves, who are now God's chosen people, of how they are to see real estate property in Palestine: "Your land must not be sold on a permanent basis, because you do not own it; it belongs to God, and you are like foreigners who are allowed to make use of it" (Leviticus 25:23, TEV).

This kind of seeing alters our perception of the land we live on (and think we own). Then "the landscape has a way of . . . giving us an awareness of our dependence on God."[10] Then all that is beneath us and around us becomes a gift given by God, and the grace of this gift begins to wash away the layers of selfish protectionism and pride of ownership. We are free to appreciate creation and the divine hand that holds it all in existence.[11]

This exuberant awareness permeates the hymns and prayers of the Hebrew people:

> How clearly the sky reveals God's Glory!
> How plainly it shows what [God] has done!
> Each day announces it to the following day;
>   each night repeats it to the next.
> No speech or words are used,
>   no sound is heard;
> yet their message goes out to all the world
>   and is heard to the ends of the earth.
> —Psalm 19:1-5 (TEV)

> Where can I go from your spirit?
>   Or where can I flee from your presence? . . .
> For it was you who formed my inward parts;
>   you knit me together in my mother's womb.
> I praise you, for I am fearfully and wonderfully made. . . .
>   My frame was not hidden from you,
> when I was being made in secret. . . .
> Your eyes beheld my unformed substance.
> —Psalm 139:7, 13-16

. . . in the New Testament Community

In his letter to the believers in Rome, Paul writes the following:

> What can be known about God is plain . . . because God has shown it. . . . Ever since the creation of the world his eternal power and divine nature, invisible though they are, have been understood and seen through the things he has made.
> —Romans 1:19-20

However, Paul also points out our tendency toward blindness to this truth about God. We ignore God's creative initiative and God's care in creation and tend to see what is around us through a clouded lens of human making. This nonseeing has given rise to a domination and abuse of the earth that many now regret. Paul's words express our greed and misuse of the earth's resources: we exchange the truth about God for a lie and worship and serve the creature rather than the Creator, who is blessed forever. (See Romans 1:25.)

Paul also speaks to the deep suffering present in creation. In Eden the earth and all creation lost its purpose and became a slave to decay and in revolt against God. In the present time, creation is "groaning in labor pains," waiting to be set free from death and decay. The same God, who created the world and all that is in it, will make all things new. (See Romans 8:18-22.)

John, an exile on the lonely island of Patmos, sees what will be and announces it to those of us who live in a creation filled with the love and grandeur of God and yet a creation that groans and suffers the tragic results of sin:

> Then I saw a new heaven and a new earth; for the first heaven and the first earth had passed away. . . . And I heard a loud voice from the throne saying,
> "See, the home of God is among mortals.
> He will dwell with them as their God;
> they will be his peoples,
> and God himself will be with them;
> he will wipe every tear from their eyes.
> Death will be no more;
> mourning and crying and pain will be no more,
> for the first things have passed away."
> And the one who was seated on the throne said, "See, I am making all things new."
>
> —Revelation 21:1, 3-5

. . . in the early church

With the inrush of the new thing God is doing in and through the life, death, and resurrection of Jesus, the focus of thought and action could be seen as less earthy and more heaven-centered in the New Testament and in the early church. However, with careful reflection we notice that Jesus grounds his teaching in the earth: seeing God's kingdom within images of soil and seeds, mother hens and sheep, bread and water, birds and flowers. All the created world becomes a place to discover God and the kingdom as we gaze with the help of the Spirit.

Many of the hymns of praise and thanksgiving that we sing invite us to worship as we become aware of God's care and love in creation.

> To Francis everything in him and around him was a gift from his Father in Heaven. . . . Even a piece of earth was cause for rejoicing, and he thanked God always for everything that was. He held everything to his heart with the enthusiasm of a child surprised by some unexpected toy. The air he breathed, the sounds he heard, the sights and smells of all the world entered his grateful soul through senses perfected by gratitude and purity of heart.
>
> . . . He wanted to tell the trees and flowers, the animals and birds, the streams and rivers, the hills and plains how wonderful they were, and how much joy to [people] and praise to God they gave, just by being there. . . .
>
> And he was not worried or anxious about yesterday, today, or tomorrow because Christ is, and all things are in Him and He is in the Father. Francis no longer worried, not because he was a naive optimist, but because he had become in prayer and penance a realist who saw the unimportance of everything but God, and in God and with Him and through Him, the importance of everything. God was everywhere and His presence charged creation with a power and glory that made everything shine with beauty and goodness in Francis' eyes.[12]

Out of his joy and wonder at God's goodness in creation, and possibly with Psalm 148 in mind, Francis wrote a hymn of praise:

Highest, all powerful, good Lord,
Yours is the praise, the glory and the honor,
And every blessing.
They belong to You alone,
And no [one] is worthy to speak Your Name.

So, praised be You, My Lord, in all Your creatures,
Especially Sir Brother Sun,
Who makes the day and enlightens us through You.
He is lovely and radiant and grand;
And he heralds You, his Most High Lord.

Praised be You, my Lord, for Sister Moon
And for the stars.
You have hung them in heaven shining and precious and fair
And praise to You, my Lord, in Brother Wind,
In air and cloud, calm, and every weather
That sustains your creatures.

Praised be You, my Lord, for Sister Water,
So very useful, humble, precious, and chaste.

Yes, and praise to You, my Lord, for Brother Fire.
Through him You illumine our night,
And he is handsome and merry, robust and strong.

Praised be You, my Lord, for our Sister, Mother Earth,
Who nourishes us and teaches us,
Bringing forth all kinds of fruits and colored flowers
and herbs.

O, and praise to You, my Lord,
For those who forgive one another in Your love
And who bear sickness and trials,
Blessed are they who live on in peace,
For they will be crowned by You, Most High!

Praise to You, my Lord, for our Sister bodily death,
From whom no living man [or woman] may escape:
How dreadful for those who die in sin,
How lovely for those who are found in Your Most Holy Will,
For the second death can do them no harm.

O praise and bless my Lord,
Thank Him and serve Him
Humbly but grandly![13]

This hymn, which Francis wrote in 1225, we still sing today: "All creatures of our God and King, lift up your voice and with us sing, O praise ye! alleluia!"

INVITATION TO PRESENCE

☘

PRACTICING: SEEING GOD'S CARE IN CREATION

Bring something from God's creation into your house or apartment this week: maybe a plant or some flowers, a bird feather, some soil or some fruit, sea shells or some stones. Allow this gift from God to remind you of God's presence and care as you begin to pray.

If possible, go for a walk outside. Walk slowly or just sit in the open and bask in the creation around you. Be present with all your senses: smell, touch, hearing, taste, and seeing. Immerse yourself in what you see, and open your spirit to receive what creation is saying about God's presence and care.

JOURNALING

You may want to draw what you see or write a few sentences of what you saw and heard as you contemplated creation.

☘ What did you notice?

✤ What did you "hear," however slightly?
✤ What is your response to God now?

BACK ON THE PATH

✤

During the week, continue to open your attention to the creation around you. If you are unable to go out into the open, you may find one of the following suggestions helpful:

. . . Choose a picture of a landscape or of something in God's gift of creation. Allow yourself to be still and open, receptive to God's presence and care.

. . . Sit comfortably by a window and gaze upon what you can see—the trees, the sky, birds, flowers, hills, fields.

. . . Read the hymn of Saint Francis slowly, allowing yourself to see each part of creation he mentions with your imagination. Stay with any scene that particularly draws you, and be open to God's presence and care there.

. . . Sing a favorite stanza from the hymn "All creatures of our God and King," and allow the words to sink deeply into your heart. See what the hymn is describing. Open yourself to God as you contemplate creation in the hymn.

This week, open your attention to creation all around you. To help you see, carry the words of the psalm with you: *The earth, O Lord, is full of your steadfast love.*

ENDNOTES

1. Phil Kniss; used with permission. Phil shared this experience with other pastors at Eastern Mennonite Seminary.
2. John Nolland, *Word Biblical Commentary*, vol. 35b: Luke 9:21–18:34 (Dallas, TX: Word Books, 1993) 687.
3. Ibid., 685.

4. Canon Leon Morris, *The Gospel According to St. Luke*, Tyndale New Testament Commentaries (Grand Rapids, MI: William B. Eerdmans Publishing Co., 1974), 213.
5. Annie Dillard, *Pilgrim at Tinker Creek* (New York: Harper's Magazine Press, 1974), 202.
6. Ibid.
7. Ibid., 203. Dillard, a contemplative writer, explains that this view of matter is based on "The Principle of Indeterminacy," which holds that we cannot know both the velocity and position of a particle of the atom at the same time. Once the position is determined, the velocity "blurs into vagueness; or you can determine the velocity, but whoops, there goes the position." What scientists are saying now is that something else is at work at the very core of matter—something with free will, with a "mind" of its own. The scriptures say it this way: Jesus Christ . . . "by him all things in heaven and on earth were created, things visible and invisible . . . by him all things hold together" (Colossians 1:16, 17).
8. The Greek word *katanoeo* means "to immerse oneself in [an object] and hence to apprehend it in its whole compass." New Testament usage emphasizes visual immersion—perceiving with the eyes. "This sensual perception or contemplation mediates impressions which can be points of contact for the attaining of important religious or ethical insights." See Gerhard Kittel, ed., *Theological Dictionary of the New Testament,* vol. IV (Grand Rapids, MI: William B. Eerdmans Publishing Co., 1967), 975.
9. Tannehill, *The Sword of His Mouth*, 60–67, quoted by Nolland, *Word Biblical Commentary*, 692.
10. Wayne Simsic, "The Landscape and Spirituality," *Spiritual Life* (Spring, 1988): 36.
11. David B. Burrell, "John of the Cross and 'Creation Spirituality,'" *Spiritual Life* (Fall, 1991): 174.
12. Murray Bodo, *Francis: The Journey and the Dream* (Cincinnati, OH: St. Anthony Messenger Press, 1972), 31–32.
13. Ibid., 147–49.

FOR FURTHER READING

Bodo, Murray. *Francis: The Journey and the Dream.* Cincinnati: OH: St. Anthony Messenger Press, 1988.
Contains insights into many situations that fret us all today.

Foster, Richard J. *Celebration of Discipline: The Path to Spiritual Growth.* San Francisco, CA: HarperSanFrancisco, 1988.
Contains a good chapter on simplicity. See also *Freedom of Simplicity* by the same author.

O'Connor, Elizabeth. *Letters to Scattered Pilgrims.* San Francisco, CA: HarperSanFrancisco, 1982.
O'Connor includes two letters on money and manages to help us uncover how our personal histories shape our decisions and attitudes toward money and its use.

9

SEEING GOD IN ALL THINGS: WITHIN OURSELVES

Pay careful and wholesome attention as you work to complete your salvation, because God is the One who is at work in you, enabling you to desire and to do God's pleasure.
—Philippians 2:12-13, author's paraphrase

I remember standing for the closing hymn. I was still conscious of my new white dress and shoes, glad to be dressed like my friends who also had reaffirmed the baptismal vows our parents and godparents had made for us when we were infants. The bishop had asked us, "Do you reaffirm your renunciation of evil?" And we had all responded, "I do."

"Do you renew your commitment to Jesus Christ?" And I had responded along with the others, "I do, and with God's grace I will follow him as my Savior and Lord."

After the renewal of our bap-

tismal vows, covenant, and another prayer, the bishop walked over to where we stood and laid his hand on each of us. I remember his hand's resting lightly on my head—my hair freshly shampooed and clean for the occasion (so important when one is thirteen). At the same time the words of advice the vicar had given us during confirmation classes came to mind: "Don't expect anything to happen when the bishop lays his hands on you. No lightning is going to strike. But do remember that his laying on of hands is a sign that you are empowered with the Holy Spirit as you choose to follow Jesus."

Well, when the minister says words like those, what is a young teenager supposed to expect? After all, something might just happen . . . But as the bishop prayed I felt nothing except the lightness of his hand as he prayed, "Strengthen, O Lord, your servant Wendy with your Holy Spirit; empower her for your service; and sustain her all the days of her life. Amen." [1]

But God was present and working within me. As I began singing the closing hymn I became aware of the words. My white dress, my friends, the bishop's hand on my head, all faded into the background as I sang,

> *O Jesus, I have promised*
> *To serve Thee to the end;*
> *Be Thou forever near me,*
> *My Master and my Friend.*

A clarity came within me. I saw myself more clearly, with an honesty I did not usually experience. I sensed somehow that Jesus was inviting me to follow him, but I knew I could not do that. I didn't have whatever it took to follow and to serve him all the way to the end. And at the same time I did not really want him as my Master and my Friend. It would cost too much. I wasn't ready. I felt longing and resistance.

I had no idea that God was at work in me, that the Holy Spirit was showing me the homely and the true about myself. No, there was no lightning, nothing dramatic or spectacular. But the Holy Spirit was responding to the prayer of the bishop (and doubtless the prayers of others), assisting me to see myself in the light of Jesus and his invitation to follow him and know him as Master and Friend. That work would continue, and after two more years of God's patient calling and help, I was ready to say "yes."

❁

Only then did I recognize more clearly the way God had been working in my life to bring me to a faith commitment in Jesus. However it did not occur to me that I could pay attention to God's presence and working in my life. I knew I should pray and read scripture, attend church, and figure out what I should do with my life. No one mentioned the part of the Christian life that emphasized the enjoyment of God's presence and guidance as to how God works in one's life.

We in the church are becoming aware of a deep inner hunger for something more. It has to do with a hunger of the spirit and the satisfaction that only God can bring. At the same time we wonder how we can live a life of faithful discipleship, growing and maturing in Christ. This pilgrimage calls us to pay attention to Jesus' invitation to see, to discern what is of God with the help of the Spirit, the scriptures, and the believing community.

Reflection
Look back over your own faith journey, and notice your openness to God, your resistance to God.

WALK INTO THE FIELD

✿

SEEING WITH JESUS

After intense days of teaching, healing, and providing for the needs of thousands of men, women, and children; and being pursued with interrogation from Jerusalem's religious leaders, Jesus and his disciples spend some time in retreat. In the spacious silence of the slopes of Mount Hermon, north of Lake Galilee, Jesus invites his followers to reflect on their experience of the last few days.

Matthew also invites us into the mountains for a time of reflective discernment along with the disciples. Like them we have been busy, on the move. In the quiet Jesus helps us be open and aware of God's presence and work and recognize our responses.

God's work is in and through Jesus, and so this wise rabbi begins with a question about himself: "Who do people say that the Son of Man is?" (Matthew 16:13). The disciples answer, "Some say John the Baptist, but others Elijah, and still others Jeremiah or one of the prophets" (Matthew 16:14).

Having heard the answers that emerge from a pluralistic and confused community, Jesus now asks a much more personal question: "But who do you say that I am?" (Matthew 16:15). It is one thing to know what other people think and say. We hear all kinds of opinions about Jesus. Now Jesus asks us to discern our own response.

One of the disciples speaks up. Simon Peter responds, "You are the Messiah, the Son of the living God" (Matthew 16:16). The lesson in discernment continues as we listen to Jesus' response: "Blessed are you, Simon son of Jonah! For flesh and blood has not revealed this to you, but my Father in heaven"(Matthew 16:17).

The "blesseds" of Jesus' earlier sermon on the mountain echo back to us now (Matthew 5:1-11) as Jesus helps Peter know that he is blessed—a happy man—because God is at work in him, opening his eyes and helping him see who Jesus is and what Jesus is about.[2]

Apparently Jesus knows our tendency to take a spiritual truth and interpret it according to our own preferences. So he explains what the Messiah must do: "He must go to Jerusalem and undergo great suffering at the hands of the elders and chief priests and scribes, and be killed, and on the third day be raised" (Matthew 16:21).

Peter is shocked because he is sure God cannot fail and in denial because his image of the Messiah is that of a forceful political ruler (Matthew 20:21, 24; Luke 24:21; Acts 1:6). He blurts out "God forbid it, Lord! This must never happen to you" (Matthew 16:22).

Jesus now identifies the source of Peter's anxiety as he replies that God is not the only one at work within us: "Get behind me Satan! You are a stumbling block to me; for you are setting your mind not on divine things but on human things" (Matthew 16:23).

Satan, the archenemy of God is at work. Peter's misguided human nature blinds him; he cannot see God's hand in Jesus' suffering and death. Peter's desire to grasp power by military might and commercial control—a temptation Jesus faced in the wilderness (Matthew 4:8-11)—has captured his attention. Jesus recognizes the bait, the trap, and the powers at work that make the offer. Hence his rebuke and his response to Peter. Jesus clearly identifies the power that is at work within Peter's heart, as well as the symptoms of the seduction of what is against God. This kind of awareness is costly, and now Jesus makes the shape of this cost plain:

> If any want to become my followers, let them deny themselves and take up their cross and follow me. For those who want to save their life will lose it, and those who lose their

life for my sake will find it. For what will it profit them if they gain the whole world but forfeit their life? Or what will they give in return for their life?

—Matthew 16:24-26

DIGGING DEEPER

Jesus is giving us a lesson in discernment during a time apart for solitude and reflection. He is being the companion the disciples and we need; the companion who attends to the presence and work of God in our lives. Perhaps, you, like Peter, have a personal awareness of who Jesus is as Lord and Savior. But often we need someone to assist us in recognizing the work of the spirit of God within, as well as our response to that work. Here Jesus lets us know what to look for. As Margaret Guenther points out:

> The work of perception is not easy or automatic: we usually see what we want to see or expect to see. When we seek to discern the action of the Holy Spirit in our lives, we expect the dramatic, even the spectacular. . . .
>
> [We] may be quick to reject the homely, the ordinary, and the near at hand. Here the [spiritual] director can serve as a guide and teacher, gently pointing out the signs that are at once hidden and obvious.[3]

Hence Jesus begins by asking his followers who he is for them.

Discernment begins as we notice God's enlightenment. As a teenager during confirmation, I was discerning something but didn't know what. Jesus invites us to articulate our experience of faith. We see Peter doing this in the retreat in the mountains. Then Jesus comes alongside us to interpret our experience through the eyes of faith and in faithfulness to the gospel.

In the process of voicing and interpreting our experience, we—like Peter—will encounter evil. Rather than fearing evil powers—the response evil wants to evoke in us[4]—Matthew invites us to know Jesus deeply and to recognize the presence and protection of the spirit of God within us. As Paul reminds us, "At the name of Jesus every knee should bend, . . . and every tongue should confess that Jesus Christ is Lord" (Philippians 2:10, 11). We need to enlarge our worldview to see the work of God through Jesus' life, death, and resurrection as God's victory over the powers.

This work of God also frees us. However, even though this freedom comes as a gift, our limited human nature shrinks back from God's ways. Like Peter, we are self-protective. Hence Jesus' invitation to us to take up our cross. This act involves knowing ourselves—both our false self and what it wants and our true self in God, which cooperates with God through the presence of the Spirit of Jesus within and among us.

Reflection
Who is Jesus for you?

LISTENING WITH OTHERS IN THE FAITH COMMUNITY

. . . in the Hebrew Scriptures
From the beginning, the Hebrew Scriptures make it clear that discernment is not one of our best skills. Adam and Eve do not recognize the illusion spun by the serpent in Eden, and the results are catastrophic. However, the Hebrew Scriptures do not present a picture of an absentee God who has given up on us and all that is in creation. Rather, it depicts the God who comes to us—even while we are absent and not listening or seeing—and asks, "Where are you?" (Genesis 3:9).

Genesis also records our response: "I heard the sound of you in the garden, and I was afraid because I was naked; and I hid myself" (3:10). Here the relationship with the loving Creator is skewed. We have distorted our self-image and our image of God.

Jeremiah, lamenting the sorry state we are in and its cause, records what God sees,

The heart is devious above all else;
    it is perverse—
    who can understand it?
I the Lord test the mind
    and search the heart.

—Jeremiah 17:9-10

However, all is not lost—God is still ready to help. In the Hebrew
prayer book we discover a prayer written for individuals as they
come to the place of worship. The prayer assists persons in opening their attention to God. God then helps them see God for who
God is and themselves as the persons they are in God's sight:

O Lord, you have searched me and known me.
You know when I sit down and when I rise up;
    you discern my thoughts from far away.
You search out my path and my lying down,
    and are acquainted with all my ways. . . .

Where can I go from your spirit?
    Or where can I flee from your presence?
If I ascend to heaven, you are there;
    if I make my bed in Sheol, you are there.
If I take the wings of the morning
    and settle at the farthest limits of the sea,
even there your hand shall lead me,
    and your right hand shall hold me fast. . . .

For it was you who formed my inward parts;
    you knit me together in my mother's womb.
I praise you, for I am fearfully and wonderfully made. . . .
    My frame was not hidden from you,
when I was being made in secret, intricately woven. . . .
Your eyes beheld my unformed substance. . . .

Search me, O God, and know my heart;
    test me and know my thoughts.

See if there is any wicked way in me,
and lead me in the way everlasting.
—Psalm 139:1-3, 7-10, 13-16, 23-24

Here the psalmist invites God as a loving, skillful, all-seeing family doctor to look for any signs of disease, maladjustment, harmful growths, infection—anything that would spoil the health and well-being of the person coming in for a checkup.

We do well to note persons' desire to be obedient and their struggles as they encounter God. Hebrew Scriptures are full of such accounts: Moses' struggle with his own lack of self-worth when God asks him to return to Egypt and lead the Israelites out of slavery (Exodus 3–4); David's denial of womanizing and murder until Nathan the prophet confronts him (Samuel 12:1-9, 13). Out of this tragic loss of focus, David was able to write these words recorded in Psalm 51:

Have mercy on me, O God,
according to your steadfast love;
according to your abundant mercy
blot out my transgressions. . . .

You desire truth in the inward being;
therefore teach me wisdom in my secret heart.
Purge me with hyssop, and I shall be clean. . . .

Create in me a clean heart, O God,
and put a new and right spirit within me.
—Psalm 51:1, 6-7, 10

. . . in the New Testament community

God honors the request of the psalmist for a clean heart and a new and right spirit within. Before Jesus dies and leaves his followers, he tells them another Advocate, or Helper, will come to be with them: "This is the Spirit of truth, whom the world cannot receive, because it neither sees him nor knows him. You know him, because he abides with you, and he will be in you" (John 14:16-17).

The Helper is the spiritual presence in the world of Jesus who is with the Father, "an antidote to the sorrow that seizes the heart of the disciples in face of Jesus' departure and of the onslaught of persecution in the world."[5] The King James Version of the Bible also refers to the Holy Spirit as the Comforter. The New Testament writings get at something primary and deep here: our basic need for connection to God. Without this connection, we are orphans in the world. Jesus reassures us that he will not abandon us and leave us orphaned (John 14:18).

In the heat of divisive arguments over the presence and ministry of the Holy Spirit, persons have paid little attention to our need of presence, God with us (Matthew 1:23; John 14:16). Intimacy and closeness with God frightens us. Our false self knows what will happen if Jesus' spirit makes a home within our heart territory. For one thing, God will bring light into this otherwise dark and chaotic place: "For it is the God who said, 'Let light shine out of darkness,' who has shone in our hearts to give the light of the knowledge of the glory of God in the face of Jesus Christ" (2 Corinthians 4:6).

Just imagine! The same God who spoke light into the dark, formless void at creation (see Genesis 1:2-3), brings light to the dark and perverse paths of our heart. I don't pretend for an instant that such exposure is comfortable. We've been hiding since Eden. But then I remember trips to the dentist and the relief of having a cavity noticed, cleansed, and filled. I think of visits to the doctor and the relief of having some unknown malady that has lurked around in my body for days, finally diagnosed and a remedy given. And then I think of Jesus, who comes to heal our blindness and tell us God is safe: we can come home. God waits on the porch to welcome us. No matter how diseased and sinful of heart we are, God receives us, embraces us, washes us, and rejoices over our return. Then the presence of God through the Spirit within provides comfort—and only then.

Since God is present with us through the Spirit, creating something new, we can expect change. Those who need tight control over the organization of daily life and schedule will feel uncomfortable giving up control. But like Peter, we will discover that giving Jesus a place to stay in a spare room only lasts so long. Pretty soon he's taking over the whole house and has become host at the table.

If we can catch a glimpse of what is happening and why, then we can begin to appreciate the discomfort within as we adjust to the presence of the Spirit and to the growth of the new self in Jesus:

> Now the Lord is the Spirit, and where the Spirit of the Lord is, there is freedom. And all of us, . . . seeing the glory of the Lord as though reflected in a mirror, are being transformed into the same image from one degree of glory to another; for this comes from the Lord, the Spirit.
>
> —2 Corinthians 3:17-18

We become like Jesus. And the fruit of the Spirit bears out that presence and likeness:

> The fruit of the Spirit is love, joy, peace, patience, kindness, generosity, faithfulness, gentleness, and self-control. There is no law against such things. And those who belong to Christ Jesus have crucified the flesh [old self] with its passions and desires.
>
> —Galatians 5:22-24

The cross is present in fruit-bearing. A father told me of his anger toward his fifteen-year-old son. "Each time he comes in the door I am so ticked," he said. "He just doesn't seem to connect with me or with the rest of the family." In obedience to Jesus, the father began to pray about the problem. At first he prayed that God would change his son and help him reconnect with the family. But as he waited on God in silence, the man knew God was looking at how he felt within. Jesus was walking through all the rooms of his heart, and Jesus began asking how the father felt toward his son.

In the quiet of God's presence, this father saw his own anger and realized how negative his own feelings were toward his son. He told God what he was noticing and asked for forgiveness and help in loving. In a few days he noticed a difference in the way he felt toward his son; his son's quietness did not bother him as much. But he also noticed that his son was beginning to talk more too.

... in the early church and beyond

A form of confession has always existed in the church, and we still use it in our hymns and worship today. Over the years, believers have also sought other ways to hold one another accountable for their life of faith and love in obedience to Jesus. The development of monastic communities in the desert—and later the city—was a response to the church's need after the Roman emperor Constantine declared Christianity the state religion of the Roman empire in the early fourth century.

Out of the Reformation in the sixteenth century a new awareness emerged of the need to be faithful in our presence and walk before God. The Anabaptists stressed the need to follow Jesus in all of life. Ignatius of Loyola developed a spiritual discipline called the Consciousness Examen (an examination of consciousness) as part of the spiritual exercises he lived and taught. He designed this spiritual discipline to help persons grow in their awareness of and faithfulness to God. A more modern term is "seeing God in all things." Our spiritual discipline this week will use Consciousness Examen to focus on God's work within our lives. Next week, we will include the more outward movement of the discipline.

INVITATION TO PRESENCE

✿

PRACTICING: SEEING GOD IN ALL THINGS—WITHIN OURSELVES

Spend a few minutes relaxing and opening your presence to yourself and to God. Ask the Holy Spirit to help you see your day (the last twenty-four hours, or the past week) as God does. Look back over the past twenty-four hours/days. Let the events unfold. and pass before you. Let your feelings about the day(s) surface. Be sensitive to what is happening within you, to how you sense God is inviting you to take notice and respond. One of the following questions may be all you need for your reflection:

✿ What emerges? What do I notice, even slightly? What do I see that causes me to be grateful?

✿ What do I see that causes me to be anxious, angry, sad, fearful, guilty?

✿ In what ways did I notice God today? Did I meet God in my anxiety, anger, sadness, fear, guilt? Or did I miss God at those times?

✿ How have I cooperated with God today? not cooperated?

✿ How is God asking me to respond to God's love and work in me?

JOURNALING

✿ Which insight had particular significance for me?

✿ What surfaced that I need to stay with, pray about again?

✿ What did I become aware of within myself, or how God is at work in my life?

BACK ON THE PATH

❀

During the week spend some time in your place for prayer with this spiritual discipline. To promote your own awareness as you are working, driving, or in motion, pause at noon each day and ask,

> Lord, where have I met you?
> Where have I missed you?
> Where have I moved with you today?

ENDNOTES

1. From the service of Confirmation, *The Book of Common Prayer* (New York: Oxford University Press, 1990), 418.
2. "Blessed" is the usual translation of the Greek *makarios*, an adjective which means "happy." Jesus takes this word that usually applies to outward prosperity and transforms its meaning as he sets it in a much larger and higher plane. See John 20:29, "Happy are those who have not seen and yet have come to believe." See also Matthew 5:1-11. From Archibald Thomas Robertson, *Pictures in the New Testament*, vol.1, (New York: Harper & Brothers, 1930), 38–39, 130–31.
3. Margaret Guenther, *Holy Listening: The Art of Spiritual Direction* (Boston: Cowley Publications, 1992), 44.
4. See Richard Foster's *Prayer: Finding the Heart's True Home* (San Francisco, CA: HarperSanFrancisco, 1992) for some treatment of this subject of encountering and dealing with evil in prayer. Also Henri J. M. Nouwen's *The Way of the Heart* (San Francisco, CA: HarperSan Francisco, 1991).
5. Raymond E. Brown, *The Gospel According to John* (xiii–xxi) The Anchor Bible (Garden City, NY: Doubleday & Co., Inc., 1970), 714.

FOR FURTHER READING

Barry, William A. *Finding God in All Things: A Companion to the Spiritual Exercises of St. Ignatius.* Notre Dame, IN: Ave Maria Press, 1991.

A helpful and fresh approach to experiencing the spiritual exercises of Ignatius and to finding God in everyday life.

O'Connor, Elizabeth. *Search for Silence.* San Diego, CA: LuraMedia, 1986.

A helpful book containing readings, exercises and meditations on confession, and prayer for the inward and outward journey.

10

Seeing God in All Things: In Others and the World

Remembering before our God and Father your work of faith and labor of love and steadfastness of hope in our Lord Jesus Christ.
—1 Thessalonians 1:3

*D*ave sat down at the kitchen table, thankful for a hot cup of coffee and some time of quiet before the day began. His housemate and coworker George had gone to the health clinic early, before daylight. A note propped up against the cereal box read, "Flu is deadly this time around. The Kosack babies are both real bad. See you later."

Glad for the solitude, Dave leaned back in his chair and began to pray. He welcomed the half-hour available to be with God before wading into the long lines of patients at the clinic. He did love the work *though. Finally his medical studies were over, and he could begin making a difference in the world.* Lord, help me to see you here, in the city, *he prayed.*

Dave looked over toward the open window. To his surprise someone was standing on the back porch—an old man, probably in his seventies, his face white with four-days' worth of whiskers, his head as bald as an egg, and his mouth spread in a grin that revealed at least four teeth missing.

"'Ullo," the man said, still smiling.

Suddenly Dave felt angry and invaded. What did this guy think he was doing standing there looking through his window? What about privacy? What about respect? And what about his need for quiet before the day began?

"What do you want?" Even Dave was surprised at the curtness of his voice.

"Nothin'" the man replied, unruffled by Dave's hostility. "I jis thought you'd like s'm fresh doughnuts. Saw you move in, I did, an' I think the world o' George an' what ya'll does at the clinic, God bless you. See here, have somethin' with your coffee." With that he held out a sack of freshly made doughnuts, still grinning from ear to ear.

Dave stood up and walked over toward the man.

"Thanks," he said rather stiffly. "I like doughnuts."

"Sure thing," said the visitor, and after handing Dave the sack, he turned and walked off the porch.

After eating a couple of glazed doughnuts, Dave sat and looked at the sack on the table. The words of his prayer came back to him: Lord, help me to see you here, in the city. *"Was that you, Lord?" he asked.*

As he sat with the question for a while, Dave began to notice a shift within himself. "God, you are the one at work, aren't you? And the people here—you're in them too. I missed seeing that earlier. I didn't even ask that old guy his name. And here I thought I had come to make a contribu-

tion! First thing you know, someone's giving me breakfast and blessing me too!"

❀

Jesus knows that as we answer his call to follow, we bring with us all kinds of self-serving motives that blind us to seeing others in the true light of the gospel. Throughout the Gospel accounts, we discover Jesus,. assisting his disciples and other religiously minded individuals to appreciate and welcome persons whom they— and we—are otherwise quick to question, judge, and reject.

Walk into the Field

❀

Seeing with Jesus

Jesus and the disciples are on the road south into Jerusalem. The quiet days in the mountains are behind them, and Jesus knows what is ahead.

> The Son of Man is to be betrayed into human hands, and they will kill him, and three days after being killed, he will rise again. But they did not understand what he was saying and were afraid to ask him.
>
> —Mark 9:31-32

Jesus' words puzzle and worry the disciples. They cannot fathom how Jesus will suffer and at the same time triumph. These followers still expect Jesus to become the messiah-king who will restore God's order through political power. They even argue among themselves as to who will hold the highest position in the new order. In response, Jesus says,

> "Whoever wants to be first must be last of all and servant of all." Then he took a little child and put it among them; and

taking it in his arms, he said to them, "Whoever welcomes
one such child in my name welcomes me, and whoever welcomes me welcomes not me but the one who sent me."

—Mark 9:35-37

Reflection

Imagine that you are with the disciples as Jesus holds a little child
in his arms. Look at the child and at Jesus. What happens to your
desires for power and prestige? Who do you see in the child?
What are your responses to children?

The disciples are still unaware of how their will to power blinds
their receptivity to God in others. John mentions seeing someone
who was casting out demons and using the name of Jesus.

"We tried to stop him, because he was not following us."
But Jesus said, "Do not stop him; for no one who does a
deed of power in my name will be able soon afterward to
speak evil of me. Whoever is not against us is for us. For
truly I tell you, whoever gives you a cup of water to drink
because you bear the name of Christ will by no means lose
the reward."

—Mark 9:38-41

Jesus is inviting us to be hospitable—not to be the host who provides everything all the time but to create an open and receptive
space within and around us for God's work in others. This kind of
receptivity does not happen without our becoming aware of the
prejudices that we carry within us. When Simon the Pharisee
invites Jesus to dinner, the fact that Jesus allows a woman of the
city with questionable reputation to touch him disturbs Simon.

And a woman in the city, who was a sinner, having learned
that he was eating in the Pharisee's house, brought an
alabaster jar of ointment. She stood behind him at his feet,
weeping, and began to bathe his feet with her tears and to

dry them with her hair. Then she continued kissing his feet and anointing them with the ointment. . . . Jesus spoke up and said to him, "Simon, I have something to say to you."

—Luke 7:37-38, 40

First Jesus tells a short story about persons in debt being forgiven by their creditors and asks which debtor will love his creditor more, the one forgiven five hundred days' wages or the one forgiven fifty. Jesus affirms Simon when he responds: "I suppose the one for whom he canceled the greater debt." But now Jesus goes further; he knows that although Simon loves God and wants to be obedient, he does not understand God's welcome of the prodigal who comes home. Simon cannot see the gracious work and presence of God in the woman as she weeps at Jesus' feet. In response to Simon's critical and skewed judgment Jesus says,

Do you see this woman? I entered your house; you gave me no water for my feet, but she has bathed my feet with her tears. . . . You gave me no kiss, but from the time I came in she has not stopped kissing my feet. You did not anoint my head with oil, but she has anointed my feet with ointment. Therefore, I tell you, her sins, which were many, have been forgiven; hence she has shown great love. But the one to whom little is forgiven, loves little."

—Luke 7:44-47

Then Jesus turns to the woman and says, "Your sins are forgiven. . . . Your faith has saved you; go in peace" (Luke 7:50).

DIGGING DEEPER

Here Jesus invites us to look from another angle, to notice how he sees the people around him. He knows we get caught sitting in the blind corners of religious and cultural traditions, arranging and labeling persons accordingly. Luke never tells us the woman's name. We only know her by her label: "A woman . . . who was a sinner."

Simon could only see her from his corner—and withdraw accordingly. She had a reputation and so was to be avoided. Most of us have some of Simon within us. Margaret Guenther notes that we are "people of good taste who play by the rules. (The Pharisee, after all, invited Jesus to eat with him.) But also like Simon, [we] cannot believe that God could be guilty of bad taste or poor judgment."[1]

Moving to a different place of seeing means leaving the vantage point offered by the rules of society. Sitting beside Jesus can get messy, especially when women, men, and children come and weep all over our feet. This is the kind of hospitality to which Jesus invites us. In time we may come to understand that tears are a language of the Spirit and the heart. Tears often accompany grief, insight, turning and repentance, and joy. First we need to become hospitable to our own tears and to receive what they are saying, then we are less likely to judge weeping as some weak expression of uncontrolled emotion that we should control in order to be adult and mature. Then we can begin to notice the presence and movement of God in others as they come close and want us to sit with them as they weep.

This is the hospitality to which Jesus invites us. As we begin to notice Jesus' presence and perceive how God is at work in our own lives, our eyes will be opened to grace and love, and we will begin to see God at work in others.

Reflection
In what ways do you see your own tears? the weeping of others?

LISTENING WITH OTHERS IN THE FAITH COMMUNITY

. . . in the Hebrew Scriptures
The writer of First Samuel invites us to join a little family as they make their way toward Shiloh, a center for worship some eighteen miles west of their home in the hills. Elkanah has two wives. One of the women Peninnah has children but shows no patience

for Hannah who is childless. Elkanah tries to reassure Hannah of his love for her, but she becomes more and more depressed as the years go by.

Now they are making the journey again, and Hannah knows she will be worshiping the God who has not given her a child.[2] After arriving in Shiloh Hannah, tired from the trip, does not join the family for the customary meal. Lonely and harassed, she weeps out her grief. Elkanah's attempts to comfort her are of no help.

Finally Hannah enters the place of worship and opens her attention to God. In her distress and anguish, she weeps as she prays a silent prayer of the heart. She asks the Lord to see her misery, to remember her, and to give her a baby boy. In turn she vows to give this little boy back to God. Her silent praying and weeping continue for a while and catch the attention of the priest Eli.

> Eli observed her mouth. Hannah was praying silently; only her lips moved, but her voice was not heard; therefore Eli thought she was drunk. So Eli said to her, "How long will you make a drunken spectacle of yourself? Put away your wine." But Hannah answered, "No, my lord, I am a woman deeply troubled; I have drunk neither wine nor strong drink, but I have been pouring out my soul before the Lord. Do not regard your servant as a worthless woman, for I have been speaking out of my great anxiety and vexation all this time."
>
> —1 Samuel 1:12-16

Eli the priest sees this woman and makes a judgment. One might think a priest could discern the spiritual and heart needs of those who come to pray. Instead Eli judges Hannah through the distorted lens of his own understanding without asking what her needs or circumstances are. He condemns her for being drunk and making a spectacle of herself. To her credit, Hannah can explain her distraught state. Only then does Eli see her in a new light and respond with a prayer of peace and consolation: "Go in peace; the God of Israel grant the petition you have made to him."

Eli's change of heart grows out of a change of perception; with this sight, Eli receives insight. God grants grace and kindness to the heart of the old priest, which Eli can then extend to Hannah. She does not know if she will have a child, but she feels heard and comforted. Hannah then "went to her quarters, ate and drank with her husband, and her countenance was sad no longer" (1 Samuel 1:18).

Seeing with the eyes of the Spirit changes our own heart response. It can help us not only perceive God's presence but cooperate with God's gracious work within others.

Reflection
Who are the Elis in your life? Who are those persons who have either misunderstood or heard your heart's longings? What feelings do these memories evoke?

The way God works may not always be popular. Laws may even defy God's gift of life and God's way of doing things. The king of Egypt told the Hebrew midwives who assisted the Hebrew women as they gave birth during the long years of Israelite slavery, "When you act as midwives to the Hebrew women, and see them on the birthstool, if it is a boy, kill him; but if it is a girl, she shall live" (Exodus 1:16).

But when Shiphrah and Puah see the women giving birth, their reverence for God causes them to revere life. With courage born of clear-sightedness, "[these midwives] stand as guardians over the Exodus story and—ultimately—over our story."[3] Our spiritual history would not be the same had these women decided to see as the king saw!

. . . in the New Testament community
Among the believers in the church in Jerusalem Luke introduces us to Barnabas. Like the Hebrew midwives who receive brief mention and yet play a vital role in the life of the Israelite people,

Luke does not say a great deal about Barnabas. But without him large events in the history of the church may never have happened. His name means "Son of encouragement," the name given to Barnabas by the apostles because of his ability both to perceive God's activity in people and to encourage the birthing of the Spirit's presence in fruitful living.

Barnabas is the person who can perceive the reality of faith in Saul, the Pharisee who had persecuted believers around Jerusalem, hauling them off to jail and having some put to death. None of the believers wanted to trust the rumor going around that Saul was one of them. It is Barnabas who sits down with Saul and listens to his story, "how on the road he had seen the Lord, who had spoken to him, and how in Damascus he had spoken boldly in the name of Jesus"—even endangering his own life. (Read Acts 9:20-25.)

It is through this listening to the person's experience—always told in story—that the formerly hidden becomes visible. We begin to see and to hear God on the move. Out of this kind of listening, Barnabas brings Saul to the apostles and they accept him among the believing community in Jerusalem. We are more galvanized in our corners in the church than we realize, and we often are slow to recognize God's presence and work in persons whom we would rather avoid.

Saul is outspoken, critical, gifted in his ability to argue and prove from the Hebrew Scriptures that Jesus is the Messiah. He is not a comfortable person to have around. His presence causes uproar, bringing more persecution for the church. The Jerusalem believers finally ship Saul off to Tarsus; he attracts too much negative attention and disrupts the peace. (Read Acts 9:30-31.)

When a newly emerging congregation of Greek and Jewish origin comes to the attention of the apostles in Jerusalem, they send Barnabas to listen to the fledgling church in Antioch on the Mediterranean coast. Barnabas listens to the story of how this group began. Believers who fled Jerusalem during the earlier persecution of Stephen, which Saul had condoned, had traveled up the coast telling others about Jesus as they went. In Antioch Greeks had believed also and turned to the Lord. What a dilemma—non-Jews in the church? Yet Barnabas delights in seeing the grace of God at work and goes off to Tarsus to find Saul.

There is more to this move to find Saul than meets the eye at first glance. Saul is the Pharisee who was behind the death of Stephen and who instigated the persecution that forced some of these believers in Antioch to leave their homes and families in Jerusalem. A greater peace comes about as Barnabas brings the former persecutor of the church to serve the persons he has wronged. The one who listens closely to our stories and the stories of others is able to see God on the move and so becomes the peacemaker among us.

Of course the story does not stop there. Next we discover Barnabas's listening to the life story of a young man named John Mark—much to the consternation of Saul, who is now Paul. Persons could label Mark a quitter, and Paul had no patience with him. But Barnabas can see God at work in Mark, and he encourages the giftedness and work of God to blossom into life and maturity by inviting Mark to travel with him as he continues to preach and teach about Jesus.

Later Paul would acknowledge that Barnabas was right. Even the person who has been heard and known by such as Barnabas may not immediately see his own need to hear and see the presence of God in others.

Reflection
Who is the Barnabas who listens to your story?

. . . in the early church
Barnabas is one who listens to another's experience and who assists that one to see God in his or her experience. He then encourages the person to live out that calling in fidelity to the

gospel. The work of Barnabas is really the task of the believing community. Within the early church this work of listening, seeing, and discerning was the ministry of testing the spirits. (See 1 Thessalonians 5:16-22; 1 John 4:1-6.) Rather than being seen as strange or otherworldly, a prayerful and wholesome awareness of what is happening is needful and life-giving. Barnabas gives us some helpful windows into seeing the value of being a good and hospitable listener and discerner.

Early in the fourth century, the Constantinian decision to declare the Christian church as the state church in the Roman Empire opened the doors of the church to everyone—pagan and Christian alike. Discerning the presence and work of God was more difficult. Distinctions blurred; values changed. In the solitude of the wilderness and desert, believers sought to hear and see more clearly what it meant to believe in Jesus and to follow him in all of life. The persons helping others listen and discern became known for their wise and humble counsel. Like signposts that give direction in the desert beyond the city and in the desert of the heart, these men and women became known as "spiritual directors."

The label "spiritual director" can cause much consternation, but it is the old classical term used to describe Barnabas's ministry and the ministry that the New Testament writers call discernment of spirits. Today we see a renewal of this ancient ministry due in part to the questions people are asking about faith, God, prayer, and their own spiritual experience. In a pluralistic society that offers many "spiritual roads" and in a materialistic society where the spiritual dimension of life is no longer validated, how do we find our way? Who gives us direction?

God's work within and among us today fosters the return of this ministry of spiritual direction. The spiritual director is not a director

in the sense that the director is the one who tells the other what to do or how to do it. To the extent that there is a director in one's life of faith, that director is always and everywhere the Holy Spirit. Our much more modest role is as helper, enabler, as others discover or establish direction in their own lives. . . . a relationship that does whatever it can to facilitate God's own direction of us in our lives.[4]

As we listen deeply to one another, hear our stories, and become aware of God's presence in and among us as well as our response to God's presence and work—we are doing the work of spiritual direction. We are being the gift of a midwife, a Barnabas to one another. And who knows what God is up to in the ongoing life and story of the church as we serve in this way?

INVITATION TO PRESENCE

❀

PRACTICING: SEEING GOD IN ALL THINGS
IN OTHERS AND THE WORLD

Be still now. Rest your body, releasing any tension. Your body is a good friend and servant. Appreciate this gift as you open your attention to God. Ask the Holy Spirit to help you see all of life as God sees.

Look back over the past day. Let the events unfold and pass before you. What emerges? What persons or events stand out for you? What attitudes do you notice within yourself?
. . . anxiety, anger, sadness, fear, guilt, hostility
. . . faith (your response to God)
. . . hope (your response in the face of difficulties)
. . . love (your attitude and response to others)
In what ways did you meet God in those feelings? Whose story did you hear today? In what ways are you aware of God in another/others?

Be in the presence of Jesus now, bringing the needs of yourself and the persons you have listened to, have noticed. End this meditation by simply being present for Jesus. Rest.

JOURNALING

Which insight had particular significance for you? What surfaced that you need to stay with, pray about again?

BACK ON THE PATH

❀

During the week spend some time in your place of prayer with this spiritual discipline. For your own awareness as you work, drive, move, pause during your day and ask,

Lord, where have I met you?

Where have I missed you?

Where have I moved with you today?

ENDNOTES

1. Guenther, *Holy Listening, The Art of Spiritual Direction* (Boston: Cowley Publications, 1992), 49.

2. Hebrew culture understood the ability to bear children to be a sign of God's blessing. See Genesis 1:28; Deuteronomy 28:4. An inability to bear children came to mean that a woman was in some way cursed or disgraced. See Luke 1:24–25.

3. Guenther, 82.

4. Dyckman and Carroll, *Inviting the Mystic, Supporting the Prophet* (New York: Paulist Press), 20–21.

FOR FURTHER READING

Barry, William A. *God's Passionate Desire . . . and Our Response.* Notre Dame, IN: Ave Maria Press, 1993.

A book that helps the reader move outward into the world in response to God's love and presence.

Barry, William A. and William J. Connolly. *The Practice of Spiritual Direction.* San Francisco, CA: HarperSanFrancisco, 1982.

A guidebook for persons interested in spiritual direction.

Bondi, Roberta C. *To Pray and to Love.* Minneapolis, MN: Augsburg Fortress Press, 1991.

A book about prayer and living in mutuality with God.

Dyckman, Katharine Marie, and L. Patrick Carroll. *Inviting the Mystic, Supporting the Prophet.* New York: Paulist Press, 1981.

A practical book that gives guidance for the inward journey of prayer, faithful living out of the gospel, and listening to the inward and outward journey of others.

Edwards, Tilden. *Spiritual Friend: Reclaiming the Gift of Spiritual Direction.* New York: Paulist Press, 1980.

Helpful information for the special friendship of support and guidance that one Christian can give another.

Guenther, Margaret. *Holy Listening: The Art of Spiritual Direction.* Boston, MA: Cowley Publications, 1992.

A "warm, untechnical and thoroughly contemporary guide to spiritual direction," well illustrated by Guenther's own experience as a spiritual director who is also a woman, wife, mother, teacher, and priest. A helpful chapter on listening to women.

Johnson, Ben C. *Speaking of God: Evangelism as Initial Spiritual Guidance.* Louisville, KY: Westminster/John Knox Press, 1991.

Brings evangelism and spiritual direction together, recognizing God's active presence in the world that draws persons to faith.

Miller, Wendy. *Learning to Listen: A Basic Guide for Spiritual Friends.* Nashville, TN: Upper Room Books, 1993.

An introductory guide for persons desiring to share their faith journey and story with one another or in a small group. Includes some guidance for spiritual disciplines along with the reading guide for Matthew's Gospel.